TEMPLAR

Paul Ivison

Lewis Masonic

NON NOBIS, DOMINE, NON NOBIS, SED TUO NOMINI DA GLORIAM

"IF SOME AMONG THEM ARE INNOCENT, IT IS EXPEDIENT THAT THEY SHOULD BE ASSAYED LIKE GOLD IN THE FURNACE AND PURGED BY PROPER JUDICIAL EXAMINATION."

ROYAL LETTER OPENING THE ENQUIRY INTO THE KNIGHTS TEMPLAR

First published 1997
Reprinted 2005

ISBN (10) 0 85318 217 5
ISBN (13) 978 0 85318 217 7

All rights reserved. No part of this book may be reproduced or transmitted in any form or by any means, electronic or mechanical, including photocopying, recording or by any information storage and retrieval system, without permission of the Publisher in writing.

© Paul Ivison 1997

Published by Lewis Masonic

an imprint of Ian Allan Publishing Ltd, Hersham, Surrey KT12 4RG

Printed by Ian Allan Printing Ltd, Hersham, Surrey KT12 4RG

Visit the Lewis Masonic website at:
www.lewismasonic.com

CONTENTS

ILLUSTRATIONS

CHRONOLOGY

1070 *c*	Birth of Hugues de Payens
1070	Formation of the Order of St John
1088	Election of Pope Urban II
1090	Birth of St Bernard
1095	Council of Piacenza
1096	First Crusade
1099	Fall of Jerusalem
1100	Baldwin I elected king of Outremer
1109	Stephen Harding elected Abbot of Cîteaux
1112	St Bernard arrives at Cîteaux
1113	Order of St John acknowledged by papacy
1115	St Bernard arrives at Clairvaux
1118	Baldwin II crowned king of Jerusalem
1118-9	Initial formation of the Knights Templar
1119	Charter of Charity
1120	Official recognition of the Knights Templar at Nablus
1126	Count Hugh of Champagne joins Templars
1129	Council of Troyes
1139	Templars granted leave to have their own priests

1144	Fall of Edessa to Moslems
1146	Council of Vezelay call to crusade
1147	Templars granted the right to wear red cross
1179	Outbreak of hostilities between Templars and Hospitallers
1187	Fall of Jerusalem to Saladin
1291	Fall of Acre
1302	Templars evacuate Outremer to Ruad
1307	Arrest of Templars in France
1312	Dissolution of the Templars
1314	Execution of Jacques de Molay and Geoffrey de Charney
1571	Destruction of Templar records in Cyprus

GRAND MASTERS OF THE TEMPLE OF KING SOLOMON

Hugues de Payens	1119-1136
Robert de Croan	1136-1149
Everard des Barres	1149-1152
Bernard de Tremelay	1153
Andrew de Montbard	1154-1156
Bertrand de Blancfort	1156-1169
Philip de Nablus	1169-1171
Odo de St-Amand	1171-1179
Arnold de Torroja	1181-1184
Gerald de Ridefort	1185-1189
Robert de Sable	1191-1193
Gilbert Erail	1194-1200
Philip de Plessis	1201-1209
William de Chartres	1210-1219
Peter de Montaigu	1219-1232
Armand de Perigord	1232-1246
William de Sonnac	1247-1250
Reginald de Vichiers	1250-1256
Thomas de Berard	1256-1273
William de Beaujeu	1273-1291
Theobald Gaudin	1291-1292
Jacques de Molay	1293-1314

PREFACE

As a boy I was enthralled by the legends of King Arthur and the Holy Grail, the Crusades, and the Knights Templar. As the years went by my interests changed somewhat, and I developed an obsessive interest in the French Revolution of 1789. I read and re-read whatever I could on the subject. Within the texts I found the occasional reference to a "conspiracy" theory, implying that the whole affair had been orchestrated by an underground group of conspirators. The objective of the organisation appeared to conclude with the execution of Louis XVI. It was said that, as the blade of the guillotine fell on his neck, a man ran from the crowd and dipped his kerchief in the warm blood, shouting "Jacques de Molay. You are avenged!" The name meant very little to me at the time.

Some of the main leaders of the Revolution were Freemasons, mainly belonging to the "Lodge of the Grand Orient" encouraging allegations that the root cause may have been a conspiracy. In due course I visited Paris and went on a journey of discovery. One summer's evening, as the sun set, I found myself wandering near the Isle de Paris, not far from Nôtre Dame. I saw a small stone staircase leading down to an island on the Seine. I was not drawn to it by a mystic response, I just walked down out of curiosity. I stood on the platform at the edge of the river and looked into the Seine. Deciding that there was very little of interest, I turned to go back up the stairs and as I did, noticed there was a fading bronze plaque, almost hidden by ivy on the wall of the bridge. Being naturally inquisitive I studied it. I read the words "Jacques de Molay" in the text and with my limited French, gathered that someone had died here. The name rang a bell! And it came back to me where I had read it before. I stood and reflected for a while. Despite the noise above on the bridge, it was relatively quiet. I suddenly had the sensation associated with going into an ancient cathedral. I felt I was on hallowed ground. I waited and yet nothing broke the spell. There was just the warmth of the evening and the ripple of the Seine. Some minutes later I re-emerged on the busy main road above.

My father later introduced me to Freemasonry and we talked about it as one does between father and son. In the course of conversation, he informed me that there were many other branches extending from the main core of the Craft, one of these being the masonic Knights Templar. Apart from my interest in the Craft, my thoughts went to this degree of Christian chivalry, spurred on by my interests as a boy. In the due course of time I joined Freemasonry. My ambition, if that is the correct term, was to become a Knight of the Temple. In the period that occurs between joining the Craft and being able to advance to other degrees, I read. This period coincided with the publication of the book "Holy Blood, Holy Grail", followed shortly by a whole myriad of similar books. Again the Templars were mentioned. Within the text I noticed a familiar name, "Jacques de Molay", the last Grand Master of the Knights Templar. I went on to read the interesting ideas connected with the formation of the Templars. The various theories were intriguing, to say the least. The deeper I went into the subject the more I was convinced that there was substance in these theories. I argued with vigour that there was a connection between the Craft and the disbanded warrior monks; to a certain extent convincing myself, by reading everything and anything into the overall picture. In time I was installed as a Knight of the Temple. I became even more convinced.

I started to contact people who might know about the Templars. This led me to academics and priests who, in turn, pointed me towards mediaeval historians and chroniclers. As any researcher will vouch, it also led to my pocket and time. I became enthralled. Then I made a discovery. Supposition – the danger of all would-be experts. The deeper I dug, the quicker I realised that a lot of information laid before contemporary readers on the subject of the Templars was based upon poor foundations. In part this was due to a lack of first hand information and the destruction of the Templar records. Where there is a void, fill it. That seemed to be the rule in the question of the Templars.

The Templars were a fiercely committed order of Christian monks who fought for their beliefs and created a kingdom throughout Europe and the Holy Land. Initially committed to an ideal, circumstance changed them into a mighty money-making concern which ultimately fell to a stronger, greedier power. My conclusion, at the end of much research and much debate, is that there is no connection between the Knights Templar, Freemasonry, or any conspiracy theories that may run through history. Unless, that is, something else comes to the fore.

The only hypothesis I present is that the Order may have been the idea of one St Stephen Harding and his young protégé, St Bernard, who, in Citeaux, saw the need for a Christian militia based upon the Cistercian Order of monks. Nothing more mysterious than that.

Even without this hypothesis, the Order of the Temple was based upon the Cistercian Order. Therefore, upon its cornerstone, the tale must begin.

In time I found out what became of Jacques de Molay, the last Grand Master of the Order of the Knights Templar and a man described as a bit of a fool in the eyes of history. But, in the final reckoning, he stood firm and recanted his confession, proclaiming the innocence of the Order and suffering terribly at the hands of his executioners. If you get a chance, visit the Isle des Javiaux and reflect. Those of you that are Knight Templars, remember him in your preceptories and your prayers.

This book is therefore in part dedicated to his memory, and of Geoffrey de Charney, the preceptor of Normandy, Hugues de Payens and all the knights, sergeants and other brethren of the Temple.

I would also like to dedicate this book to my father, who introduced me to Freemasonry.

My thanks to Professor Malcolm Barber of the University of Reading and Doctor Jonathan Philips of the Royal Holloway, University of London for their advice; William Harding;

Beverley Webb; and Laura Matthews. Finally, and most importantly to my wife Serica and our son Tom, for their tolerance and understanding regarding my time management at home whilst still completing a full day's work.

INTRODUCTION

"*In 1118, nineteen years after the fall of Jerusalem to Christian hands, nine Knights arrived at the court of King Baudoin II (commonly referred to as Baldwin), ruler of the new kingdom. These Knights were led by one Hugues de Payens, a member of the lower nobility of Champagne. The Knights stated that their mission was to protect the Pilgrims en route to the Holy Places of Jesus, and they had taken vows of Poverty, Chastity and Obedience to the teachings of Christ.*"

Most documents on the Order of the Knights Templar begin with a similar statement to the above, which in essence is true, but not totally correct. There are two major problems in tracing the history of the Order. Firstly, one encounters bias in writers of the time; secondly, the Order's records were destroyed and as a consequence this has resulted in an element of conjecture by contemporary writers.

Unfortunately, chroniclers writing at the time of the Order's formation did not record this momentous occasion, little realising the impact that the Knights Templar would have, not only on the Holy Land, but also on the social and economic development of Europe. One of the earliest and most quoted chroniclers of the Order was William, Archbishop of Tyre, who was born in 1130, some ten years after the Order was founded. Although William wrote accurately about events in the Holy Land his writings are tinged with a strong dislike for the Order. Moreover, his information comes most definitely second-hand regarding the formation of the Order, and is quoted as being biased according to which way the wind was blowing at the time. Judging by his distaste for nearly everything the Templars achieved, it is highly unlikely that he had communicated with them at all to ascertain their beginnings. Another chronicler Walter Map, is quoted as being "unreliable" and also wrote some years after the Templars' foundation. There is also Matthew Paris, who chronicled the mid-term of events in the Holy Land. His information is mostly third-hand and he wrote at a distance from England. There are other minor chroniclers, but none have yet been found who are able to fill this first and very important gap.

By the very nature of the organisation, the Templars would have kept comprehensive and accurate records. But unfortunately fate has deprived us of most of these vital historical insights. The Templar records were partly destroyed when the armies of Islam conquered the Crusader Kingdom, and when the Templars themselves took pre-emptive action just prior to their arrest in 1307. Finally, in 1571 the Ottoman Turks set fire to the vast remainder of Templar records when they invaded Cyprus.

In the centuries that followed, when the Knights Templar faded into folklore, historians, writers and mystics have tried to fill the yawning gaps. This has resulted in conjecture and supposition which, in turn, has bred more of the same until the true facts have been obscured.

There are many questions which will remain unanswered, even in those facts that have been established. These facts are based upon records that can be substantiated through available archives. The questions that do arise are for the reader to ponder and reach his or her own conclusions.

This book is a short history, written with the intention of giving a readable account of the Order of the Knights Templar – to give an insight into the individual and the organisation, without getting too bogged down in dates and references. I wish partly to dispel some of the myths, and to finally vindicate the Order with regards to the allegations made against it. I have purposely not gone into any depth regarding their part in the Crusades, since this is not the purpose of the book. If the reader is interested in the Templars and the Crusades, then I recommend that he refers to the bibliography and takes advantage of some of the excellent writings on the subject.

So let us begin our journey with an open mind.

THE SCENE

*P*ause just for an instant; let your mind drift in time away from the modern world, with its marvels of communication and its everyday wonders which we so readily accept and take for granted.

Close your eyes; step back across the gulf of time to the advent of the Middle Ages.

As the mist clears imagine yourself in a barren wasteland, surrounded by desolate brown hills denied of all greenery, with interminable paths of dust, strewn with boulders, brush and dead wood. The searing heat causes the air to be so dry that it is painful to breathe, as you suffer discomfort and pain intensified by the merciless sun beating down on your burnt and dehydrated body. Your senses are assaulted by the sight and smell of both human and animal carcasses, left to the offensive attentions of scavenging birds of prey.

The broken remains of wagons and their owners' possessions are scattered in the all pervading dust, guarded by obscene black-coated vultures who have no fear of the approach of their next meal. There is an awful feeling of doom that eats away at your mind as you continue on, knowing that every hill and turn in the road may conceal the barbaric cruelty of an enemy who has no compassion, and an unsurpassed aptitude for the application of a protracted and excruciating death.

The only motivation you have for this endless suffering is to walk in the way of our Lord, go where He went and see what He saw, to rest near to His final resting place, attain redemption for your sins and achieve everlasting life in the world to come. Your goal – Jerusalem.

It was in this atmosphere of desolation, fear and piety that the Holy Order of Knights Templar was established.

THE WHITE MONKS

*N*ear Porlock in Dorset, southwest England, some years prior to 1100, Stephen Harding was born. Apart from this fact very little is known of the early life of one of mediaeval Europe's significant saints. History, in fact, has tended to overlook this man who set out the foundation for the Cistercian Order of monks. The only description of him passed down to us is that he was "good looking in the Lord", approachable, popular, a competent bible scholar and strong organiser.

The early part of his life that can be traced shows that he began his religious vocation as a student in the Benedictine monastery of Sherborne in Dorset. In the due course of time, he completed his studies and returned to the secular world. As with most young men he was not sure which way his path in life would lead him: would he become a Benedictine monk or would he chose some other occupation which utilised the skills he had achieved from his privileged education? It has been suggested that he in fact joined the monastery as a monk before returning to secular life. Stephen travelled first to Scotland then onto France, where he settled in Paris. This was one of the great learning centres of Europe and, as one would expect, Stephen took advantage of this by studying the liberal arts. How he managed financially is not known, he may have had a personal dowry or sponsorship. Stephen completed his studies and (in the company of a friend) travelled through Europe. Their destination was Rome. On this leg of their wanderings they visited as many monasteries as they could, reciting the complete Psalter daily. Stephen quickly learnt the inadequacies of the monastic system. He became disillusioned with the observances which to him had no reason or divine authority. He also took a strong dislike to the advantages the system took with regards to the impoverished countryside. Especially monastic Orders that depended on poor communities for their creature comforts. When returning through France, both travellers came across a wooded area at Molesme in the Burgundy region. To their surprise they came upon a small community of monks. The friends stayed for a number of days. Stephen became impressed with the commitment of this group of brothers. They were trying to achieve a life of total self-sufficiency. Their life was poor, but they worked hard to produce enough vegetables to exist. The work routine was interrupted at regular intervals for prayer and this appealed to Stephen's austere nature. Stephen had found his niche. Bidding his friend farewell, he stayed at Molesme.

Some years had passed by when Stephen decided to leave, with twenty other brothers. They approached the Papal legate in France and begged to be released from their vows and continue their religious devotions elsewhere. This was granted and they founded the Abbey of Cîteaux, where Stephen became prior. Here they continued in the spirit of the Benedictine Order. Their life was just as austere as before, but worse since they had to start afresh with nothing.

In 1109 the abbot died and Stephen was elected in his place. His regime became even more severe. He refused to accept any support whatsoever from outside the monastery, and ordered the removal of anything that was not functional. The emphasis was upon prayer and manual labour. During this period he was instrumental in setting out the initial format for the Cistercian Rule. This involved the total rejection of all personal luxuries, as well as the use of feudal sources such as peasant labour, millers and blacksmiths. In addition, any lay brothers who were dependent upon the local community were excluded. As time went on the numbers of monks diminished. Word had spread of the hardship endured at Cîteaux, which discouraged the influx of any novices. Monks died and there was no fresh blood. Starvation and disease began to take its toll. After three years of dedication and hard work, the Abbey and Stephen's regime were close to destruction. Stephen prayed for the impossible, a miracle. In answer to his prayer, a young man arrived at the wooden gates of the Abbey one morning. With him were thirty of his friends. They approached Stephen and asked permission to join the Abbey. Stephen was somewhat surprised since the young man and his companions were of noble birth, totally unused to the severe lifestyle that existed at Cîteaux. The abbot gladly welcomed them. Thus in the year 1112 Bernard, the third son of Tescelin Sorrel of Burgundy, came to Cîteaux.

Bernard was born at Fontaines, near Dijon in 1090, one of six children. Both parents were kind and caring to noble and serf alike. His mother, Aleth, was Bernard's earliest influence. She was a woman of beauty and extremely devoted to her religious beliefs. Bernard is described as an aggressive, self-righteous young man of slight build. In due course of time he adopted a shaved crown and a sparse brown beard, similar to most religious men of the era. Due to his frugal lifestyle he suffered from severe stomach problems, which plagued him throughout his life. In the early years of manhood Bernard retained the doctrine of his class. He believed in the feudal system and his position within it. This position ensured that he adopted the ideals of chivalry and the qualities of knighthood: courtesy, honour, the defence of the weak and the way of the warrior. However, the latter was offset by his religious upbringing, the basis of which was the Benedictine doctrine, renowned for their scholarship. Bernard was educated in grammar, logic and rhetoric. His studies led him to examine the Jewish religion and its complex folklore. Through education and self-examination, and a search for a meaning to his life, this persuasive young man found himself outside the gates of Cîteaux with thirty of his associates.

Stephen, the master, and his disciple, Bernard, set about the foundation and development of the Cistercian Order, based upon the Benedictine doctrine. What better combination for the task than an effective organiser and a charismatic young man full of the ideals of religious youth?

What did they plan together, the old man who once set forth on a journey of self-sufficiency and the man of twenty two with a privileged upbringing? Ultimately what they produced was the format for the Cistercian Order, a religious order of monks who were totally self-sufficient within society and the eyes of the Lord. They led a simple lifestyle and became efficient civil engineers. They were able to develop the most barren wasteland with their knowledge and skills. The Cistercians were especially adept in the supply of water. (The word cistern derives from the Order.) They played an important part in the development of early agriculture and sheep farming, which later led to their influence in the wool trade.

One is bound to question whether Stephen and Bernard envisaged a Christian utopia. They did. This is borne out by the nature of their philosophy, which was essentially the cleansing of feudal life through religion. But, encompassed in this, did the abbot and his chivalrous protégé envisage the need for a Christian militia, fighting for God and the survival of the Christian world, in the wake of heresy and Islam? Presumably, if the Cistercians were able to create a society that lived as God intended, then they would need an army to protect them. Both Stephen and Bernard were well-travelled men and understood the mediaeval world and all its hazards. Or were they both far sighted enough to see a future need for a dedicated Christian force? Unfortunately, history at this point has not yielded any documentation to prove this theory. This is hardly surprising since the established order would have viewed any such ideas as dangerous.

In 1115, Bernard (with the blessing of Stephen), was released from Cîteaux, possessing a Rule by which to live in order to establish a new house. Bernard chose an equally sparse and barren stretch of land situated in Clairvaux, in the vale of Absinth, Champagne. The Count of Champagne, Hugh, had gladly offered it to him. The Order grew and prospered with

Hugh's influence and Bernard's charisma. From this first Chapter grew sixty eight others, as far afield as England and Ireland. Bernard's fame and influence increased at the same time. But Stephen Harding remained in the background.

In 1119 Stephen Harding was responsible for the final chapter in the development of the Cistercian Order, the Charter of Charity. This finally defined what the spirit was in the eyes of the orthodox church. It permitted the induction of the lay fraternity into the Order, and established a system of regular visitors and general meetings for the association of Cistercian abbeys.

The Cistercian monks wore a habit of white to profess their innocence to the world.

OUTREMER

*I*n 1088, Urban II was elected Pope. He was a forty six year old Benedictine from the monastery at Cluny, in France. Ten years prior to his election, the Emperor of Byzantium, Alexius Comnenus, had declared war upon the Seljuk Turks. The Emperor needed support from the West to achieve a quick solution to his problem. His envoys conveyed this message at the Council of Piacenza in 1095. As a far-sighted Christian idealist, Urban was aware of the problems that existed with bored and belligerent warlords in Europe. Consequently he favoured the idea of sending aid from the West. Urban spoke to the crowds back home in Clermont, stating the Holy Places of Christendom were in danger and needed to be saved. The reaction to his plea was greater than he had anticipated. Throughout Europe thousands flocked to his call. The opportunity for plunder, the relief from everyday boredom and the offer of salvation for their sins encouraged the masses to take up the cross. By August 1096 the First Crusade had begun. By 1099 it was all over with the capture of Jerusalem. The Crusader kingdom had been won. The Holy Land was now in the possession of the Christian West.

Massacres of the local inhabitants had been rife with the advent of the Christian armies. Betrayal had been the name of the game. Anything was acceptable in the politics and warfare of the era in order to secure a victory in the name of

Christ. All would be forgiven in His name. Even the priests and holy men had committed their share of the butchery. The Moslems had never experienced such a blood bath, especially in the name of religion, and because of this could not reconcile it with their own religious beliefs. As a consequence the Crusaders were to become hated and distrusted by the surrounding kingdoms.

The first Christian king of Jerusalem was Godfrey de Bouillon (Boulogne), who was aged about thirty seven when he seized the kingdom of Jerusalem. The crusaders called the Holy Land *Outremer* (pronounced *Outre mare*, which means beyond the sea or lapis lazuli, a semi precious stone of deep blue). With him was his brother Baldwin, who had been bound for a life in the Church, but had laid the Church aside and taken the cross as a soldier. Baldwin had married an English woman, Godehilde, who followed at his side throughout the First Crusade. Godfrey was the perfect Christian knight and Baldwin attempted to emulate his brother. However, Baldwin had a penchant for the fineries of life. Upon his brother's death, his younger brother seized the crown and became Baldwin I.

The new king was crowned in 1100 at Bethlehem. He had the magnitude and credibility required of him, including a beard to match. He was aware of, and interested in, the affairs of his new found kingdom. His energy was boundless, loathing laziness, in both lords and subjects. He ruled by example and upheld the virtues of Christian chivalry, making him popular with friend and foe. Baldwin addressed internal problems from belligerent princes and, in his short reign, attempted to secure his kingdom, which he achieved with relative success. However, he died of poisoning, from a fish caught in the Nile whilst out on expedition with some of his knights.

In any struggling kingdom the death of the king will send it into a state of severe insecurity, especially when surrounded by an enemy intent upon its destruction. On 2nd April 1118, King Baldwin I died. The new king, Baldwin II, nephew of Godfrey, ascended a very fragile throne. He was known as the Goad (something that torments or spurs into action by being irritating). He was described as pedantic, suspicious, cautious and constantly at prayer. Some would say paranoid. Not a particularly favourable state to find himself, especially in a changeable environment such as Outremer, where the fortunes of an individual could change from one extreme to another in a matter of hours. A serf could become a knight overnight and vice versa.

From Baghdad, Ascalon, Tyre and Damascus, the realm faced the threat of invasion. It would appear that the death of Baldwin I was the trigger for the Templars. The leading cleric of Jerusalem, the Patriarch, wrote letters to the West begging support from the Christian kings. In particular he asked for more men, money and food. The crisis was at its worst when there was both a concerted offensive on Jerusalem and an attack upon 700 pilgrims, of which 300 were killed and about 60 taken into slavery. Despite the obvious necessity to deal with the threat to Jerusalem, the question of protection for the pilgrims was just as important since the kingdom would flounder without them.

The stage was now set for the formation of the Knights Templar. The pilgrims needed more protection than ever before and Outremer was in desperate need of a disciplined and dedicated army to defend it. The Crusader armies were usually on a short term contract and apt to return home as soon as they had completed their term or fulfilled their penance. In Jerusalem there was a small lay confraternity of penitent veterans from the First Crusade. These one-time warriors had taken the oath of chastity, poverty and obedience. They were sworn before the Patriarch of Jerusalem, Warmund of Picardy, who was the spiritual head of the Church, ranking in jurisdiction immediately below the Pope.

Very little is known of its structure and its establishment. The official history of the Order states there were nine knights, a figure that has caused much debate. Another figure that has been offered is thirty. The latter has a much more sensible ring to it, but both figures should be considered. The brothers were part of the army from the First Crusade and nine may have been knights. The remaining twenty one could have been retainers from the camp of each knight.

These lay brothers were approached by Baldwin II, the Patriarch, and the ruling Barons of Outremer. One must consider whether this was the moment that the brothers had been waiting for in realisation of a larger plan, or whether the warrior spirit within them was awakened by the imminent destruction of the new Christian kingdom. However, regardless of the reason, under the leadership of a man called Hugues de Payens, the brothers dedicated their lives to the protection of the Holy Land and its pilgrims.

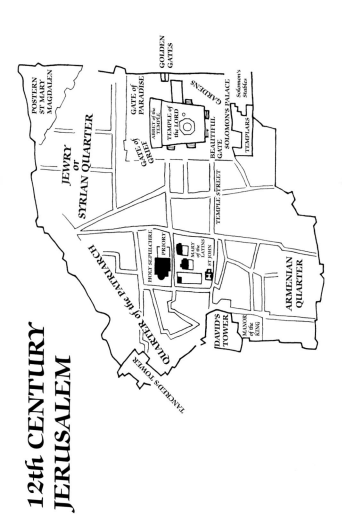

12th CENTURY JERUSALEM

POSTERN ST MARY MAGDALEN

GOLDEN GATES

GATE of PARADISE

ABBEY of the TEMPLE

TEMPLE of the LORD

GARDENS

Solomon's Stables

JEWRY or SYRIAN QUARTER

GATE of GRIEF

BEAUTIFUL GATE

SOLOMON'S PALACE

TEMPLARS

QUARTER of the PATRIARCH

TEMPLE STREET

HOLY SEPULCHRE

PRIORY

MARY of the LATINS

ST JOHN

ARMENIAN QUARTER

TANCRED'S TOWER

DAVID'S TOWER

MANOR of the KING

Baldwin gave the new order accommodation at the south end of the threshing floor of Mount Moriah and to the south of the Dome of the Rock in Jerusalem, above the supposed location of the stables of King Solomon. Today, this area houses the al-Aqsa Mosque. As a further boon, he allocated a small square adjoining the west side of the Mosque for their monastic offices. From this gift they took their name, The Poor Fellow Soldiers of Christ and of the Temple of King Solomon. In time this became the Knights of the Temple and, finally, the Knights Templar.

The crisis in Outremer had still not been solved. The ruling powers finally came together to discuss possible solutions at Nablus, the ancient capital of Samaria (once called Shechem, about thirty miles north of Jerusalem), on the 23rd of January 1120. They were there not only to debate Outremer in crisis, but also to deal with affairs of state. On this day the Order of the Knights Templar was officially accepted, under the command of the first Grand Master, Hugues de Payens.

A MAN OF LITTLE IMPORTANCE?

*W*hat is known about this man, Hugues de Payens? Yet again very little, in view of his importance. Records are few and far between, due partly to his position in society. A young man of noble birth who was also the eldest son of a large dynasty would have great things expected of him. His early life would, therefore, be chronicled for future generations. However, if he was a younger son or of lower nobility then less would be expected of him. As a result the years before his fame would be largely ignored and unrecorded. An example of this is King John of England, who was overshadowed by his brother Richard I. Much of John's early life is unknown. During the crusades many minor individuals suddenly came to prominence when very little had been known about them previously. Hugues was one of these. (This might also explain the lack of information concerning both Stephen Harding and St Bernard.)

Hugues de Payens was born around the year 1070 in the village of Payens, which is about eight miles from Troyes, within the province of Champagne (today it is part of the department of Aube). His coat of arms was purported to be three black heads upon a field of gold. At the age of twenty five he fought in the First Crusade. It has always been stated that he was a member of the lower nobility of Champagne, part of the old aristocracy whose specific tasks were to accompany their liege lord on military campaigns and witness any decree that emanated from the courts of the said lord. Interestingly enough, his name appears on a charter as a witness to grants made at Molesme.

He is described as being totally dedicated to his responsibilities and totally merciless in any matters concerning his beliefs. But there was another side to him too. He was regarded as being good-natured and caring in many respects, especially to his fellow Christians. Within Hugues we see the true personification of the Templar. The perfect ideal of the Christian warrior; kind and loving to those of the faith, and totally ruthless to the enemies of Christendom.

Hugues' relationship with his liege lord, Count Hugh of Champagne, was slightly incongruous. Albeit that he was from the lower nobility, they were close. From the limited information available it has been ascertained that Hugues was friendly with a number of influential members of the aristocracy in the area. There have even been suggestions that he was related to Count Hugh of Champagne. The consensus is that he was part of an inner circle of friends of the count, and his family may have had more influence than the records show. They do indicate that his family may have been lords of castles at Isles, Pont sur Seine, Troyes à Estissac, Montigny Onjon and Bois de St Mary near Cerilly. Hugues was married and had a son called Theobald, who later became abbot of St Colombe de Sens. It is thought that the death of his wife may be one reason for him taking up the cross.

After the First Crusade, both Hugues and his liege lord made a pilgrimage together to the Holy Land in 1104, both returning and are recorded as being in France in 1113. However Hugues later returned to the Holy Land in 1116. The reason is not recorded, and once again Hugues returned to France. The rest is even more vague, but it seems that he then returned shortly afterwards to form the lay confraternity that set the basis for the Order of the Templar.

Between the years of 1104 and the formation of the Templars there is a lot of coming and going on the account of Hugues. Why? Was there a reason?

When examining the formation of the Order and the status it quickly rose to, it is quite understandable. Hugues, although a member of the minor aristocracy, was surrounded by a host of highly influential friends from one of the most powerful provinces of France. Nearly everything of importance concerning the early development of the Order emanates from Champagne.

Upon the official formation of the Order, the village of Payens was granted a commanderie of Knights Templar, possibly as a mark of respect to the founder.

THE EARLY YEARS

*T*he names of the founding knights are: Hugues de Payens, Geoffrey St Omer, Payen de Montdidier, Archambault de St Aignan, Andre de Montbard, Godefroy Bisol, Roral, and Gondemare. By tradition there is a ninth, but history does not reveal his name.

The fledgling Order struggled to exist. Clearly the commencement of the Templars was not a very momentous occasion in the everyday life of the Holy Land. The impression given is that the matter had been considered, a decision had been taken and then, like most good ideas, forgotten. The once noble knights of the fledgling Order ceased to wash, and grew their beards in an act of penance. The brothers had no formal attire and dressed in anything they could find. This was generally discarded clothing or that given to them. Their eating habits left a lot to be desired, considering they were a fighting force. Most of the time they were near starving and, as before, had to rely on charity or anything they could scavenge. It would appear the small enclave tried to be as little of a burden to the populace, yet the brothers could not survive without them. Moreover, they seemed to have trusted in the Lord to aid them in their mission. Possibly in the adage: The Lord will provide. Their raggedness was reflected in the environs of the Temple at Jerusalem, which had become very faded. It is no wonder they were first known as The Poor Fellow Soldiers of Christ and the Temple of Solomon. Reputations in the Holy Land were easily forged, but the Templars were slow in the ascendance. In the year 1120 they had a new recruit, Fulk, Count of Anjou. But he was only an associate member. This meant he was only on a fixed term contract and would later return to his normal life. In 1126 Count Hugh of Champagne joined the Order as a fully operative member and now answered to his former vassal, Hugues de Payens.

On this point many have surmised that there may have been a mysterious reason. However, what is rarely acknowledged is that the Count had a domestic problem. Even earlier, in 1114, Hugh of Champagne had fled East to escape it. He suffered from an overbearing wife, whom he hated! This highly probable reason for his joining the Templars is never mentioned as it would not fit in with the fanciful ideas that abound. St Bernard condoned this move by Hugh, but added he was a little bit upset the Count had not joined the Cistercians!

Records yield little regarding achievements by the Poor Knights of the Temple during the nine years following their foundation.

TROYES

"*T*he ninth year from the beginning" was how Jean Michael, the scribe who recorded the text of the council at Troyes, described the length of time that the Order had been in existence. The New Year in France was always on the 25th of March. Bearing this in mind there is an anomaly in the dates given by historians. The official date given throughout history is 1127. However, bearing in mind the problems of the New Year and the decision at Nablus in 1120, it would appear that the council at Troyes sat on the 13th of January 1129. (For further information on this see Malcolm Barber's book "The New Knighthood".) This date can also be verified by evidence from various contemporary charters.

After the apparently hasty formation of the Knights of the Temple and their growing importance in the Holy Land, there was a need to have official sanction from the Holy See. In effect, they needed a Rule by which to govern their secular life. Baldwin II had written a letter to St Bernard asking for help in this matter, and this was delivered personally by one of the founding knights, Andre de Montbard, Bernard's uncle. Bernard reacted favourably and swiftly to the plea, for reasons we will probably never know. There are questions that present themselves. Did this appeal to the religiously utopian ideas of Bernard? Was he able to foresee the need for an established Christian militia in the future? Or was this all part of an ideal that had begun with Molesme? We can only guess. Whatever the reasons, the new Order gained the support of the most powerful voice in Christendom. Bernard courted the Pope, Honorius II, who convened the council at Troyes to consider the suggestion. On a very cold day in the cathedral in Troyes, one cardinal, two archbishops, ten bishops and seven abbots sat to debate the issue at hand. One of the abbots was the somewhat shadowy figure of Stephen Harding. Sat upon a bench writing was John Michael. Apart from the religious hierarchy the crowd consisted of laymen and other less important clergy who sat and listened. Amongst them was Thibauld, Count of Champagne, soon to have his own problems with his liege lord, Louis VII, King of France. Thibauld had just recently inherited his title from his uncle Hugh, who was now a full serving brother in the Templars.

Before the semi-circle of religious leaders stood Hugues de Payens, supported by five of the founding brothers of the Order. Brothers Geoffrey (St Omer), Roral, Payen de Montdidier, Godefroy Bisol, Archambault de St Aignan. These "knights" appeared odd to say the least. People were used to seeing tidy coiffured men with jewels and fine clothes, not the six men before them with their long dirty beards, cropped hair and tattered cast-off clothes.

Interestingly enough, Jean Michael records that "The same Master Hugues with his followers related to the above-named fathers the customs and observances of their humble beginnings and of the one who said: ego principium qui et loquor vobis, that is to say: I who speak to you am the beginning, according to one's memory." This statement does strike one as odd. By implication it is saying that there was someone present other than Hugues and his brothers who was the founder of the Order. Hugues recounted the history of the Order and its aims. To conclude, he begged for recognition from the Church, money, more men and a rule by which to regulate their life. The secular authorities considered the argument put forward and the adoption of a Rule based upon the brainchild of Stephen Harding and St Bernard, "The White Monks" i.e., the Cistercian Order. It was granted.

In all there were seventy two clauses. It was stipulated there were to be no women in the Order to ensure chastity. The knights were to wear white as a symbol of chastity, and possibly also in recognition of its Cistercian foundations. The grade below knight was the serving brother or sergeant. Their garments were to be brown or black mantles. This did not mean they were less chaste, but signified their lower status. Married men were allowed to enter the Order, generally on a short term contract. However, even if a knight, they could not wear the mantle of white. The Rule further judged that as they were knights they could have lands, castles and servants. It went on to set out their daily life with regard to eating, prayer, and absenteeism. Even their bedding and pastimes were addressed. To ensure that all candidates were sincere in their applications to the Order, a vetting system was introduced. This was followed by an elaborate initiation ceremony which was specifically laid down. After initiation each new entrant completed a probationary period. Out of this intricate document came a totally ordered and communal lifestyle, creating a discipline for which the Templars became famous.

It was at Troyes that they were granted their first gift of land.

Hugues then travelled from France to England, and on to Scotland on a recruiting drive. Young men from all over Europe thronged to join this new Order of chivalry which, in modern terms, was similar to a Foreign Legion.

With this influx of initiates came gifts of land and more wealth as it was surrendered by each new brother. So the Order grew in numbers and power. Further, at the behest of Hugues, St Bernard wrote "In praise of the New Knighthood". This acclaimed the new Order of Christian chivalry and sneered at other forms of knighthood. He wrote of salvation through the Templar life style and reconciled the contradictions of killing in the name of Christ and Christian virtues.

In 1139 the papacy gave permission for the Order to have its own chaplains, allowing it autonomy over its internal affairs and exempting it from taxation. Thus, the Order finally became a state within a state, swearing loyalty to no king (except the Spanish Templars who swore allegiance to their king), answerable only to the Grand Master and ultimately the Pope.

In a short space of time the role of the European Templars changed. To begin with they were a recruiting ground for service in the Holy Land. With extensive gifts of land and property, their duties soon became administrative. The lands had to be farmed and their produce sold. Revenues were collected and moneys invested. The primary objective was to supply the demands of the Order in Outremer. Whether it be armour, horses, food or ships, they were the lifeblood of their Eastern brothers. All the members of the Order had exactly the same Rule to live by and enjoyed the same privileges, but the two spheres were totally different. The European Templars were skilled artisans; blacksmiths, farmers, tanners, shepherds etc, from all walks of mediaeval life. They included bankers, investors and a whole spectrum of businessmen. Those in the Holy Land were full-blooded, capable warriors; the zealots of Christendom. From this it can be deduced that the Templars in Outremer were chiefly a brotherhood of knights, whereas the Templars of Europe were in the main, the complete opposite.

The three main centres in Europe were England, France and Spain. We can find evidence of the Templars' ownership of land in England by the use of the word "Temple" in its title.

In Spain much embarrassment was caused by King Alfonso I of Aragon who, seeing the potential of the Templars in the fight against the Moors, gave them a third of his lands.

To give an example of their administrative power and expertise, at one point in England there were only six knights, eleven priests and one hundred and seventeen serving brothers controlling vast tracts of land and property. This illustrates the extent of their administrative expertise, and gives testimony to their Rule and management skills. Bearing in mind that they were exempt from taxation, it is easy to see why they became at the same time so wealthy and unpopular.

In the due course of time the Order entered the sphere of mediaeval politics, an area of high intrigue and betrayal. The Order earned a reputation for trustworthiness and, thus, became the confidantes of princes and kings who were greatly influenced by their opinions. Many rulers, whilst not operative members of the Order, enjoyed its privileges and were often seen in the company of its members. Richard I of England always travelled with a complement of Templars and, on occasion, dressed himself in the clothing of the Order.

The extent of their favour can be further measured by the honour extended by King Louis IX of France. His son was born at the Templar Castle of Athlit in Syria. The king gave the Grand Master the privilege of being his child's godfather (contrary to clause 72 of the Rule, which expressly forbade any Templar to become a godparent!).

SECOND CRUSADE

here are three landmarks in the early development of the Templars; Nablus, Troyes and the Second Crusade. Strangely enough the latter was orchestrated by a now somewhat familiar figure.

At the northeastern borders of Outremer lay the Christian city of Edessa. This had fallen on the 24th of December 1144 to the Moslem army, sending shock waves through Christendom. The voice of the slightly built St Bernard was heard once again. His oratory held audiences bewitched as he called upon Europe to take up the Cross, promising total absolution to all. At Vezelay, in Northern France, on Easter Sunday 1146, Bernard's mantle fell from his shoulders and he demanded that crosses be shaped for the faithful to wear on their shoulders as a sign of commitment. Europe became a frenzy as thousands answered his call. At that moment King Louis VII of France was in the midst of an internal problem with Thibault, the Count of Champagne, which unfortunately had led to virtual civil war. Louis fell ill. Bernard berated him for his sins and his argument with Thibault, threatening him with hellfire and damnation. Louis is described as a devout Christian, but "simple". Against the advice of the court elders, Louis surrendered to these threats and took up the cross. Everard des Barres, the Master of the Temple in France, marshalled one hundred and thirty knights in support of the Crusade. At St Denis in Paris, on the 27th of April

1147, the crusaders gathered in the presence of Pope Eugenius III, King Louis VII and St Bernard. Everard des Barres and his one hundred and thirty knights accompanied them, arrayed in their white mantles. The abbot of St Denis presented the king with the battle banner of St Denis, a lance flying a blood red flag with golden flames. Eugenius, following the example of Bernard at Vezelay, granted the resplendent White Warriors of the Temple the right to wear the eight-cornered red cross on the shoulder of their mantles and upon their left breast. This was to show to all the whiteness of their purity and their willingness to shed blood in defence of Outremer.

That same year the crusaders set off on the first leg of their journey, towards Constantinople through Hungary. It was on the second part of the journey, having passed Constantinople, that the Templars demonstrated their discipline in marching and forged their reputation. Starvation set in and the army started to eat their horses. Only the Templars refrained and preserved their supplies, fully aware of the importance of cavalry when fighting the Turks. The discipline of des Barres and his brothers so impressed the leaders of the crusaders that they ordered the army to befriend the knights. With des Barres as the overall commander, he directed one of his knights, Gilbert, to set up units of fifty soldiers, led by a Templar knight, who in turn was answerable to Gilbert.

These new units were taught five basic lessons in engaging the enemy, and these became the order of tactics for future warfare in Outremer. Firstly, they would march in an orderly fashion, and not as a rabble. Secondly, there was to be no retreat until the word was given by the knight in charge, or whoever was commanding the field. Thirdly, upon withdrawing, they were to immediately regroup and reform their fighting positions. Fourthly, front units were not to advance to the rear should they perceive that it was under heavy attack, but to remain where they were. Finally, the units which flanked the main column were to remain in order and hold their position. Despite this new army, the Second Crusade was not a success. This was mainly due to the Turks' tactics of allowing their sheep to graze ahead of the advancing army, thereby scorching the earth and leaving nothing for the armies to eat. However, the Knights Templar had managed to save lives and keep the enemy at bay by presenting a solid front to the enemy, even though starvation had weakened them considerably. Christendom finally had clearly defined tactics when fighting the Moslems. This helped to forge the Templars' reputation, not only in the eyes of Christian leaders, but more importantly in those of the people of Europe. They began to see them as their means of salvation in the crusade against a terrible enemy.

The last string to their bow was added upon Louis's arrival in Antioch. The Crusade had bankrupted him, and he therefore turned to the Order for help. Everard des Barres arranged loans for him which in turn virtually bankrupted the Temple. However in performing this almost foolhardy act, des Barres helped to further raise the king's esteem for the Templars. Thus it was that from this disastrous campaign, the Order of the Knights Templar achieved status in the eyes of the Pope, the most powerful throne in Europe, and the people of

Christendom. This was to set them on their course for the next one hundred and fifty nine years.

With a firm footing in the Holy Land and influence within Europe, the Order was now able to consolidate its power base. Although their ideology was fundamentally inward-looking, they extended their influence into the outlying Islamic kingdoms. There was nothing unusual about a religious order of warriors to the world of the Moslem because they had their own. The Order practised good business sense and honoured their commitments (when it suited them). This impressed the rulers of the East, who were disillusioned with the dealings they had had with crusader leaders. The Order of the Temple became the diplomats of the West, opening vital links. For the first time, Christendom entered into talks with Islam.

STRUCTURE

*W*ithin the Order various grades of membership existed, but women were not admitted. Clause 70 of the Rule has elicited a great deal of conjecture. The wording contains "henceforth" when discussing the exclusion of women. This implies that prior to the Council of Troyes, women may have been admitted to the Order. Much later, women were employed by the Templars to help care for pilgrims. These "ladies of the Temple" took the same monastic vows of chastity, poverty and obedience as the men. However, it is certain that women were not admitted to the warrior or higher echelons of the Order. In all probability they ranked lower in status than any of their male counterparts.

At the lowest level were the servants who were known as the frères de metier, the brother craftsmen or manual labourers. They were responsible for the upkeep of the Chapter houses and associated tasks of cleaning, cooking and waiting. This level also encompassed the carpenters, masons, tanners and other craftsmen.

Parallel to this group were the brothers who were responsible for the Templar estates, such as farmers and shepherds. They were called the frères casaliers, brothers of the land.

Next in line were the esquires, whose sole responsibility was to the fighting brothers of the Order. Their duties were to care for the horses, armour and weapons, ensuring that food was in plentiful supply whilst on campaign. Though they tend to be overlooked, the esquires were in fact the backbone of the Templar army.

All the warrior ranks were far superior to those already mentioned. The lowest of these were the sergeants and serving brothers. These were all freemen and made up the cavalry and infantry ranks. They wore black brown habits adorned with the red Cross Patée. The sergeants and serving brothers out-numbered the knights by about three to one.

Then there was the knight. He is a figure conjured up in the imagination when a Templar is mentioned, wearing the white mantle of innocence adorned with the red Cross Patée. For the most part he was drawn from the lesser known aristocracy, versed in the art of war, strategy and the use of arms. Armed with a double-handed sword and double-pointed mace, he was an individual who aspired to great things and, in consequence, became a formidable fighting machine, striking fear and respect into the hearts of any foe.

Each knight had three horses and an esquire. This might seem to contradict the Great Seal which was of two knights on one horse. However one of the many explanations of this is the Seal represented the military and clerical aspect of the Templars who were tasked with one mission. The double-handed sword carried by the knights was not only a weapon, but also symbolised the omnipresent Cross. Therefore, when held reversed, it aided his meditations and gave solace to a dying brother on the field of battle.

The Templars also employed native horsemen to form light cavalry units. They were known as Turcopoles and were formed from a mixture of mercenaries and a small number of local inhabitants. The brother in charge of these groups was called the Turcopolier (in the Hospitallers this section was under the control of the English Chapter).

The estimated total of Knights Templar in the Holy Land was about six hundred knights and eighteen hundred serving brothers. The number of Turcopoles is not known but an approximate figure for the entire Templar force is two thousand six hundred. Of this number, about half were based in Jerusalem.

In battle, retreat was forbidden unless the odds were overwhelming or more than 2:1. The custom of paying ransoms for captured knights was also forbidden. However this was not strictly true since a Templar could offer the clothes he stood in, together with his loincloth in payment for freedom. Needless to say, this was not a particularly tempting offer! As a consequence the death toll was very high, and this do or die attitude could partly be responsible for their reputation for fierceness.

There were priests and clerics, and men of learning, within this hierarchy, with the ability to read and write – a great rarity in mediaeval Europe. They provided the records and accounts of the Order.

At that time, it was generally forbidden to learn any philosophy or religion other than Christianity. However, the

Knights Templar developed a reputation for their knowledge and understanding of Eastern religions and philosophies – very necessary when dabbling in espionage and the diplomacy of the Holy Land. It was the men of learning who attempted to unravel the hidden mysteries of the East which they subsequently passed on to their successors. This was a very powerful and dangerous position to adopt, and one can see why the inquisitors' allegations were believed.

The Templar priests were the custodians of a large number of "relics". These included such items as: The True Cross, a piece of wood formed into a cross that was said to have been made from a bath in which Christ had bathed; a bronze cross made from the bowl Christ had used to clean the Apostles' feet; scrapings of blood from the crucifixion and a crown of thorns which sometimes flowered. All of these were very powerful in the eyes of Christendom, and were brought out at religious festivals and in times of emergency.

When the crusaders sacked Caesarea, they recovered a beautiful chalice. It was rumoured to have belonged to Joseph of Arimathea and to have been the cup from which Christ and his disciples drank at the last supper. In all probability the story of the Holy Grail stemmed from this find. Since it was the responsibility of the Templar priest to care for most religious artefacts, it is highly likely that they were the custodians of the chalice, thus giving some credence to the legend that later arose.

In examining the structure of the Templars one anomaly clearly exists. Despite being a brotherhood of monks they still held on to a feudal ranking structure. However, in its defence, the Order was a military elite and had to retain a viable chain of command and ensure strict discipline (as well as appeal to those of higher birth!).

At warfare the Order was either spectacularly successful or an abysmal failure. Their failures were due to poor leadership locally or zealous confidence in the face of overwhelming odds. Whatever the outcome, they were respected and feared by allies and foe alike.

The Knight Templar was a hard, ruthless warrior dedicated to the glory of God, whose valour and bravery ensured him a place in history.

The language of the Order of Knights Templar was primarily French. Each member of the Order was called by his title, preceded by the word *frère*, the french for brother, or the Latin *frater*. Thus a knight would be *frère chevalier* or *frère mareschal*. This applied to all levels, even those of lower rank.

Their obedience was total and absolute. Their fidelity was to the Pope and then the Grand Master, after which followed the rank structure. They were answerable to no other authority. It is easy to understand why they were seen to pose a threat to the European royalty. Henry III of England was informed by the Master of the Order that he would only be permitted to continue his reign if he maintained justice.

The administration of their affairs was in essence quite simple and totally effective. At the head was The Grand

Chapter which was based in Jerusalem, and the main governing body. It was responsible for ensuring that all gifts of land were allotted fairly and governed correctly, with the right of veto concerning elected Masters. It was only this elected body that could authorise any decrees or alterations to the Rule, and these were senior officers appointed according to which item was to be debated, generally headed by the Master of Jerusalem, who was allowed his own treasury (the title Grand Master was a much later term). When absent the position was filled by his deputy, the Seneschal. All treaties were signed by this august body, including any major troop manoeuvres and declarations of war, which were overseen by the Mareschal who was responsible for military matters.

All the complex financial affairs of the Order were the sole responsibility of the Commander of the Kingdom of Jerusalem.

The Commander of the City of Jerusalem was in charge of the welfare of pilgrims. The Hospitaller, as is suggested by his title, oversaw any medical needs that the Order or pilgrims might have.

Another position in the hierarchy was the Draper. He ensured that the Order was properly attired for war and ceremonial occasions.

Another function of the Grand Chapter was the admission of candidates for knighthood, ensuring that appropriate checks were made as to the candidates' standing before initiation could take place.

Upon the death of a Grand Master the Grand Chapter convened. In the interim a Grand Commander was elected to oversee affairs. Nominees were proposed from the provincial Chapters and subsequently considered. When a decision had been reached the Grand Commander stood down and the new Grand Master was invested.

Below the Grand Chapter came the provincial Chapters, which would control their own respective provinces. In charge of these was a Master who, like the Grand Master, had his own treasury and in turn was answerable only to the Pope and the Grand Master. The Master was otherwise totally responsible for his own province. There were nine provinces in total: France, England, Poitou, Aragon, Portugal, Apulia, Hungary, Antioch and Tripoli.

Each province was further divided into houses, each of which had a Commander. The discipline and general running was executed by a Knight Commander, who was second in command. Thus each province and house was autonomous.

Every knight had to attend meetings unless he was ill or his duty made it impossible for him to attend. The Commander began the proceedings with an address. This was similar to the reading of minutes at a modern day formal gathering. They would discuss matters that had arisen since the previous meeting; admonishments; the current state of the house; any foreseeable military or political problems; items which would affect the basic running of the house such as food and supplies. This would be followed by the confessions of any knight who may have strayed from the Rule or committed sins before God. Due to the power invested in the house it meant that most problems could be dealt with internally and immediately for the most part. However if the matter could not be resolved quickly or involved too heinous an offence, it would then be referred to the Province or, in extreme cases, to the Grand Chapter.

Listed below are a few of the penalties according to the Rule:

Expulsion, Life imprisonment or Death

- Murder
- Treason
- Desertion
- Heresy
- Procuring entry to the Order
- Conspiring with other brothers
- Revelation of secrets / initiation ritual

Sent to stricter orders
(Benedictines/Augustines)

- Absent without leave
- Leaving the House other than by the front door
- Absent for more than two nights (without permission)

Loss of privileges for one year;
Living with the servants of the Order;
Deprived of horse, armour etc.

- Disobedience
- Contact with women
- Attempting to escape from the Order

Administration chart of the chain of command

POPE

↕

GRAND MASTER

↕

GRAND CHAPTER

↕

SENESCHAL
(Deputy Grand Master)

↕

MARESCHAL
(Responsible for military affairs)

↕

MASTER OF PROVINCE

↕

PROVINCIAL CHAPTER
(Of which there were nine)

↕

HOUSE CHAPTER

↕

COMMANDER

↕

KNIGHT COMMANDER

↕

KNIGHT
SERGEANT
MEN AT ARMS

APPEARANCE

*S*o what did this individual look like? The Templar of the East was quite unique and could therefore be recognised easily. As we have already established, a Templar was not allowed to wash since a clean body represented vanity. His head was shaven, since it was also considered vain to grow one's hair and even worse to brush it. For the same reason he was forbidden to shave his face, which resulted in a matted dirty tangle. Moreover, the beard was considered a sign of manhood in the East and demonstrated to the enemy that the bearer was a full-blooded, capable warrior.

The knight of the Eastern Chapters was usually of European extraction. However, as the Order progressed, the sergeants and serving brothers were from families that had settled in the Holy Land. Many of these had bred with the local inhabitants. This resulted in the vast majority being of mixed race, or in some cases, converts from the indigenous population. Bearing this in mind, it must have been a slight cultural shock for the Preceptories that accepted them into their care when the Templars finally retreated from Outremer and were scattered across Europe – these bronzed warriors speaking in a strange dialect and cohabiting with farmers and blacksmiths! The only thing they had in common was the Rule.

These soldiers of Christ must have been a joy to meet. Probably the military reason for this unhygienic existence was that the smell reduced the number of enemy prepared to get too close – or perhaps this was the first use of biological warfare!

However, the Templar priests were the one exception to this rule of sanitary uncleanness – they were all clean-shaven, and even wore gloves to ensure they did not come into contact with anything unclean.

What sort of person was he, this soldier of Christ? Let us consider his physique. Fasting was strictly forbidden. In fact, brothers who indulged in this penance were ridiculed by their fellow monks. A weak man on the field of battle was of no use to the Lord. His frame would have been wiry and honed, bronzed from a life under the sun. Daily exercise helped to ensure he was skilled in the art of warfare. Whether using the lance, sword or mace, he would readily accept pain in the name of God. His physical and mental training, together with his religious ministrations, prepared him to die fighting the good fight. His belief was sound and unshakeable. The Templar fought to the death. It comes as no surprise that Saladin, the most honourable of Islamic combatants, hated the Templars with such a venom. A brother of the Order was a zealot of the highest extreme and suffered no man. Yet when it suited him, especially in the political field, he could be considerate and a man of vast understanding. There is the tale of a Moslem who was staying with the Templars and went to pray in the Temple. A Frankish knight, new to the Holy Land, took exception to this and started to manhandle him. Very quickly a group of Templars came to the Moslem's rescue, apologising for the knight's behaviour. The perfect diplomats?

As the Templar's power base and influence spread, so did their arrogance, unfortunately spilling over into the Christian communities. In time the Pope would have to issue a bull ordering that brothers of the Temple should not be dragged from their horses and given a beating by fellow Christians. When the Order first occupied the island of Cyprus, they had to take refuge inside their castles within a week. The local inhabitants had been subjected to their arrogance and could tolerate it no more. They tried to lynch them.

KNIGHT TEMPLAR

INITIATION

"You seek what is a great thing,
but you do not know the strong precepts of the Order.
For you see us from the outside,
well dressed,
well mounted,
and well equipped.
But you cannot know the austerity of the Order.

For when you wish to be on this side of the ocean,
you will be beyond it,
and vice versa,
and when you wish to sleep,
you must be awake,
and when you wish to eat you must go hungry.

Can you bear these things for the honour of God
and the safety of your soul?"

"Knights" – A. Hopkins

The perfect Templar church was circular, to emulate the Holy Sepulchre. However, they were not all built in this way. These buildings were sparsely decorated with little in the way of furniture, reflecting their sworn poverty and abhorrence of vanity. When conducting services of worship, in common with many other monastic orders, the Templars did not kneel, but stood.

Initiation ceremonies were always held in secret, as were meetings. It is known that there were several levels of attainment, dependent upon the rank of the initiate, each one secret to those of a lower sphere. The disclosure of secrets was punishable by fines, expulsion and even death. Research has shown that the secrets referred to were within the Rule. A knight, therefore, would have greater access to the workings than a sergeant. To give an example, when reading the Rule on enemy engagement, the need for secrecy is understandable, since it would be dangerous if the information fell into the hands of the enemy. A guard was posted at the door of the meetings with either a war axe or double-handed sword, ready to dispatch any unqualified intruder or fraudulent interloper.

"The rite of introduction into a society." This short sentence is the dictionary definition of the term "initiation". In addition, the definition of a society is "the state of living in organised groups". Therefore the term "initiation", with regards to the entrance of a knight into the Order of the Temple, is perfect.

There have been many strange ideas about what exactly happened during this ceremony of induction. This has been mainly due to the belief in a hidden Rule running alongside the authorised one. Picture this – the romantic figure of a lone postulant kneeling on a dank stone floor before the altar of his God, to whom he is willing to lay down his life. The fragrance of incense permeates the air, and chants issue from an echoing chamber on hallowed ground. In the gloom, white cloaks emblazoned with red crosses, shimmer in the flickering candle light, framing the beards of warrior monks.

The romantic can have a field day! The imagination will leap ahead, especially when presented with a few morsels of gossip and lack of first-hand knowledge.

The whole ceremony is laid down, quite specifically, within the Rule. When it is read in its entirety, there is nothing untoward or mysterious.

Prior to his entrance, a knight was required to spend a night in solitude and prayer in order to reflect upon his decision and to seek forgiveness for any sins he may have committed. After completing his vigil, the Initiate was taken before the brethren of the Chapter. The assembled brothers were then asked if they knew of any reason why this man should not be admitted to the Order. If no reasons were expressed, he was taken to a another chamber. Here the candidate underwent strict examination by the Master and two or three senior officers. This was to ensure he was the correct material and that the would-be entrant was aware of the seriousness of his commitment. "Do you seek the fellowship of the Order of the Temple and share in the spiritual and temporal goods which are in it?" If the Initiate answered in the affirmative, the severity of the Order was explained to further guarantee that the knight was not joining for mercenary reasons. He had to be an unmarried man of the Catholic faith, who did not belong to the Hospitallers, Teutonic Knights or any other religious Order. One question that was always included was whether he had bribed anyone to gain admittance. After this, the Initiate was taken back to the first chamber. The assembled brothers were again asked if there was any reason why this man should not join them and if it was their wish he should become a brother of the Order. The Initiate then requested admission. After being reminded once again of the severity of the Order and his commitment, he was asked to leave the room. In his absence the assembled brothers were again asked the same question. Upon his return the same procedure was adopted.

The initiation began. The candidate knelt bare-headed before the Master, with his hands clasped together as in prayer. The four gospels were sworn on and he vowed to a life of poverty, obedience and chastity, promising never to desert the Order, to fight for the Holy City, never to own property and to protect all Christians.

The Master then took a mantle and put it around the Initiate's shoulders and tied the laces. The priest said prayers and the other brothers each recited the Lord's prayer. Then followed the ritual kiss, offered by the Master as he raised the newly-made brother from his knees. The priest then followed suit. The Initiate was then placed on a seat before the Master and the rules were explained to him, i.e., the penalties of the Order and the lifestyle he was expected to adopt. The ceremony was now complete and the new brother was welcomed into the Order.

Later he was issued with his appointments (bedding, uniform, armour and horses), in much the same way as any modern day member of the armed forces (see Appendices II and III).

The brothers of the Temple were great believers in ritual, which is borne out by their induction ceremony and the regulation of their regime. Not only did they observe a strict initiation ceremony, but also one of expulsion.

Any brother to be excluded was presented to his brothers in the Chapter House, dressed only in his britches with a rope of penitence around his neck. Kneeling before the Master, charges were read and a formal letter of dismissal was issued. The excluded brother was then advised to pray for forgiveness and the salvation of his soul. Having been suitably admonished he was sent to a stricter monastic Order, such as the Benedictines. Should he refuse, he was then placed in manacles and confined until he changed his mind.

If guilty of a lesser charge, he might lose his habit. This entailed the removal of his regular clothing, the handing in of his horses and armour, and the loss of privileges. Following this he was flogged before the assembled brethren, and this practice continued weekly for one year and a day. During this period of penitence he was banished to the confines of the lowest levels of the Templar establishment. Here he cleaned, served and assisted in all menial tasks.

At the end of his sentence the Templar was reinstated. However, all was not forgiven. He was never allowed to forget his past transgression; never being able to give advice to another brother or carry the Beauséant, let alone command brothers in the field. However strict the rules and regulations were, they were adhered to.

The Templar hierarchy was able to assert authority over its membership with strict ritual, fear of damnation, and with degrading and severe punishments. This proved to be one of their strengths in a feudal society that was haphazard, with little regard for regimentation.

LIFESTYLE

A brother could only be admitted in a state of poverty. Any wealth or property were given to the Order, from which the fraternity greatly benefited. The initiates were gathered from the lower, middle and upper echelons of mediaeval society, including lords and princes. All had to give freely and in poverty. Each initiate was allocated to a House (or Chapter). The Templars slept in dormitories, on single wooden pallets. Their only comfort was a sheet and one blanket.

In the early years of the Order eating was conducted in an atmosphere of humility and silence, with two men sharing a single bowl. Their diet was slightly better than the average freeman at that time, but meat was only allowed three times a week. Their attire was equally sparse. In the Preceptories they wore simple monks' habits without any comforts like fur.

However, in time these harsh conditions ceased, and it appears that some of the early precepts of the organisation were left by the wayside.

The knights began to eat at their own tables and were allowed a selection of meats at each meal. They were completely segregated from sergeants and esquires who dined at a different time, away from those of higher birth.

Despite these later changes the meal was still served and eaten in silence, although a priest would now read from the scriptures throughout the meal.

A Templar's working day began promptly at 4am when he arose to feed and groom his horse. He was then allowed to return to bed for a short while. Upon reawakening, the day began in earnest, starting with the celebration of mass. At 6am he attended the service of the first hour of the day, Prime. This was followed by a service at 9am, Terce. After worship, time was allowed for physical training in arms and the grooming of horses. The equipment provided for horses was basic and practical, devoid of rosettes and decoration of any kind. The saddles were also simple, made of leather with no stirrups. Hunting was considered a pleasure and was therefore strictly forbidden, with the exception of the lion.

Just before noon he celebrated the service of Sext. This was followed by lunch, at which fasting was strictly forbidden for the simple reason of keeping fit and strong. Nones was celebrated at 3pm (the ninth hour of the day), and Vespers at 6pm. After supper attendance was required at Compline, which was regarded as the last service the day. Wine and water were served after this and instructions were issued for the next day. The Templar then bedded down his horse, but he had one more duty to perform. At midnight he attended Matins, the first service of the day, at which mass was again celebrated. Finally he was allowed to retire to bed, in complete silence.

Candles were burnt all night in order to prevent any lewd behaviour in the Templar dormitories. Privacy was nonexistent, with even the Templars' letters read aloud to the assembled brothers (a Templar was not allowed to kiss a woman, not even his mother. Nor was he to appear naked in front of another Templar).

Friday was a day of penance and spent solely in prayer. Extra time to sleep was the only reward for a hard day's work.

EMBLEMS

$\mathscr{T}$he famous seal of the Templars depicts two knights riding on a single horse, and purports to represent their abject poverty. Though tasked with a divine mission, they could only muster a single horse between them. However this bore no resemblance to reality since each knight was allotted three horses. Upon the reverse side of the seal was a representation of the Dome of the Rock. Although this was primarily a Moslem house of worship, the Crusaders had quickly converted it and named it the Temple of King Solomon.

The red cross worn on the mantle of a Templar was equal-armed, expanding outwards from the centre, and mounted on a white field. The shape is known as a Cross Patée. The Cross Patée has eight corners, representing the eight beatitudes of Christ.

The other banner is more mysterious and subtle. The "Beauséant" is formed from a field equally divided horizontally into a black upper half and white lower half. It was never hung as flag, but always over a cross-bar at right-angles to the pole. The reason is quite simple – in the heat of battle it could be seen from wherever the knights were located. On ceremonial occasions the responsibility of the banner fell upon the Seneschal. In times of engagement with the enemy it fell to the Mareschal, who carried a wrapped-up spare just in case the original was destroyed. There was a strict code of conduct associated with the Beauséant. It was never to be used as a weapon. Woe betide the Mareschal, or any knight, if he mislaid it. If it was lost in the fight, then the knights were to rally to the nearest Christian pennant. The Mareschal, or knight, who carried this into battle was also referred to as the "Gonfalonier" – the Gonfalon being a banner that had been blessed by the Pope.

The interpretation of both banner and name are many and various. This in itself has helped to add mystique to the Order. The black portion of the banner is said to represent the world of sin that was left behind when the life of purity was adopted, represented by the white portion. It is also said that the white portion indicated that the knights were kind and favourable to those who followed the Christian faith, and unforgiving and merciless to all others.

Another popular interpretation is that it refers to the "Piebald Steed" in allusion to the Great Templar Seal, with two knights on one horse.

If the banner is a riddle, then the word "Beauséant" is an endless maze. Historians and linguists have toyed with the word and offered numerous explanations. Here are but a few:

The words "Á Beauseant" are said to have been one of the war cries of the Templar as he charged into battle. In an attempt to interpret the meaning of the word it may be split up, for instance:

"Á" means "To the".

"Beau" in mediaeval terms meant "noble, fair or beautiful".

"Séant" means posterior or fitting, colloquially "sit up from a lying position".

We are none the wiser, as our translation offers:

"To the noble bottom" or "To the noble correctness" or "To the noble fitting", i.e. everything that is right and fitting. Possibly "To the noble, sit up from the lying position"!

It may have been a description of how the knights sat on their horses and rode into battle – "Bien Assis" It was considered a "fair seat". This would at least explain the "noble bottom". A small lesson in not dismissing the ludicrous and laughable too quickly.

Further, the word may have been derived from the expression "Bien Assez", which means "well enough", i.e. "Time enough – let's engage".

If the word is amended to "Á Bienséant" the word translates "to the proper way".

If the word is separated into three words: 1) "Á", 2) "Beau", 3) "Séant" and the word "Séant" were to be spelt "Céant", it translates to "in this house" and we would have the war cry "To the nobility of this house". (Bearing in mind that the Templars were members of a house, or Chapter House, and there is also the possibility of an allusion to the House of the Lord.)

However in a recent publication "The Rule of the Templars", the author J. M. Upton Ward gives another spelling . . . "Baucéant". This translates "To the branch of this house". And so it goes on.

More than likely the word was just a rallying cry to the soldiers in the field. That in the heat of battle they should seek the banner.

Whatever the real meaning, if there is one, the banner is a worthy representation of the Templar. It is plain and functional with no fanciful colouring or design. It is a perfect representation of their ideology. There is no in-between, everything is black or white, i.e. Christian or not.

Their official war cry just prior to engaging the enemy was "Non nobis, Domine, non nobis, sed Tuo Nomini da gloriam" (Not to us, Master, not to our nobility, but to Thy Name give glory.)

To have heard six hundred white knights mounted on their war horses and thousands of brown-clad infantry chanting this refrain in the silence before attack, must have been awe-inspiring and terrifying to any adversary.

FINANCE

*I*n money matters the Order was unique. The Templars had connections, wealth and military power – both in Europe and the Middle East. They could, therefore, guarantee to produce funds internationally for kings and merchants alike. A sum of money paid into a Templar treasury in London would ensure the bearer of a token equal to that amount in any part of the Christian world, thus creating the basis of modern banking today. The vast majority of Templar wealth was deposited in the Temple in Paris which became the financial centre of Europe.

Ships were built to carry produce from the Order's vast holdings, military personnel and, of course, the occasional pilgrim. With help from the Venetians, renowned for their seamanship, the Templars became expert mariners in a very short space of time. This added greatly to their influence and spread of power.

PILGRIMAGE

*A*ll the major ports on the coast of Outremer were disembarkation points for Christian pilgrims. The main ones were Jaffa, Acre, Caesarea and Haifa. The route taken would invariably lead straight to Jerusalem, and then onto Jericho.

Castles were also built at strategic points in the event of attack from Moslem forces. These were generally under the command of the various Military Orders. One of the better known Templar fortifications was at Athlit approximately fifteen miles to the north of Caesarea. This was called Castel Pelerin or Pilgrims Castle.

Athlit was a popular starting point for pilgrims since they immediately came under the protection of the Templars. From here a pilgrim had to travel at least sixty five miles to the south through barren land, with little water and scant food supplies, before they reached Jerusalem. Aware of dangers from thieves and marauding bands of Moslems, the Templars created set routes with strict security. In many respects this was similar to a packaged holiday of modern times. From Athlit their journey took them south into the Valley of Ben Horon. At every point in the journey there were places where the pilgrim could purchase souvenirs concerned with either the New or Old Testaments. There were special areas of interest such as Mount Carmel to the north where the cave of Elijah could be found, Dothan where Joseph was sold by his brothers, the Tomb of John the Baptist at Samaria, Nablus the old capital of Samaria where Joseph grazed his sheep when it was known as Shechem, and many more. At the end of the Valley the route meandered up Nebi Samwil, which the Crusaders renamed Mountjoie. This was where Solomon received his gift of wisdom and was the site of the Prophet Samuel's tomb. From the top of this mountain pilgrims could see Jerusalem for the first time. God's Holy City in a heat haze, sunlight reflecting off the Dome of the Rock's golden roof. The joy they must have felt, to see their goal laid out before them.

On arrival in the Holy City a traveller would be faced with the reality. The bustle of the town with its strange smells and mixed cultures would be very different to anything he had experienced in Europe. Though naive in the ways of the East, at least he was on secure ground, protected by the omnipresent military Orders. He was now free, within the confines of the city, to sightsee at leisure. There were various tours he could choose, orchestrated by the Hospitallers, the Templars or any of the other Orders. There was the Tomb of David, the Dome of the Rock (Mount Moriah), the Garden of Gethsemane, Golgotha. He could travel outside the city to the tomb of the Virgin Mary, see the mountain where Christ was tempted, or visit Bethany where Lazarus and his sisters had lived. Here was a host of marvellous places that would prick the pilgrim's imagination. He had heard of them and now could actually touch them, bringing his soul that bit closer to God.

From Jerusalem the pilgrim might travel to Jericho, following in the steps of the Good Samaritan, then bathe in the River

Jordan. This was one of the most perilous legs of his journey. The road was treacherous, following the rocky incline of the terrain where a man might slip through fatigue and fall to his death. Water and food were in scarce supply. To add to his problems, the rocks and caves might harbour thieves or bandits.

The Templars regularly policed this area and had prepared a dedicated unit under the charge of the Commander of Jerusalem. Ten knights were kept in a state of constant readiness, usually with a complement of thirty other ranks, with sufficient supplies of food and water. Apart from this unit the Templars had built two fortresses. One was about ten miles from Jerusalem called the Red Cistern, and the other at Jericho called Quarantene. These fortresses and the troops on standby in Jerusalem illustrate the seriousness of the threat to pilgrims, and how enthusiastically the Templars took their raison d'être.

There was one further slight problem faced by the eager pilgrim: the differing opinions (more so in Jerusalem) amongst the Orders as to the sites of certain Holy Places. At times this led to a variety of locations which, in many instances, were either contradictory to one another or completely wrong. Unfortunately, safety could almost be guaranteed, but quality of information could not!

HOSPITALLERS AND THE TEMPLARS

A small group of brothers, set up by a collective of merchants from Amalfi, had betrayed the hospitality and kindness of the Egyptian ruler of Jerusalem. In the year 1070 the merchants had formed a hospice for poor travelling pilgrims. This had been sanctioned by the Moslems of Jerusalem who tended to tolerate other religions. In 1099, during the siege of the city, the Ruler had allowed all Christians to leave. The brother in charge, Gerard, had approached the crusaders with information which assisted in the downfall of the city. This led to the most horrific massacres imaginable. In return these brothers were allowed to continue their work, encouraged by the victorious crusaders. In due course they became the Order of the Hospital of St John of Jerusalem, later known as the Knights Hospitaller. They were not, as yet, a military force.

Their primary objective was the care and treatment of pilgrims. Even though the hospital was very basic at first, they tended the sick and dying as best they could (even having an obstetric ward). In return they received the gratitude of and encouragement from the fledgling kingdom. In 1113 the Order of St John gained official sanction from Pope Paschal II.

About six years later, with the election of a new Master, they appear to have deviated slightly from their main course, by beginning to take a more militant role. This probably owes much to the recently formed Templars. However their transformation into a military force was a slow process. Records indicate that they did not become a full military Order until some twenty five years later. However, they were so advanced on the administrative front that the Templars probably used them as a role model.

When comparing the two Orders their initial raisons d'être are quite distinctive; Hospitaller to care for the poor and suffering, and Templar to protect them.

The Rule of the Hospitaller was, in many respects, similar to that of the Templars, but less severe. Both Rules stipulated the relationship they could have with one another – they were brothers no matter what. They could eat with together since both Orders were reliant on each other in times of hardship. Should a knight or brother from either Order become detached from his unit in the heat of battle, he should seek the banner of the other Order and make his way to their lines. When they fought side by side they were a magnificent example of a disciplined mediaeval army.

But, like many theories, the realities were very different. Their Rules did not take account of human nature and political ambitions. Both were greedy for land, wealth and influence, resulting in arrogance and irresponsible competition. Their methods were not exactly in the Christian mould, with both Orders employing fraud, intrigue and murder to achieve their ends. Once the Hospitallers had fully developed as an organisation, their relationship totally soured. In fact it broke down almost irretrievably.

Visually the Templars made an impressive sight, flamboyantly dressed in their white flowing cloaks adorned with a blood red cross, invigorated with their war-like mission. On the other hand, the Hospitallers were dressed in sombre colours of black and white. They were never as wealthy as the Templars, and their army was smaller as a whole. The Hospitallers were considered more staid in attitude and lifestyle; their mission almost boring in comparison. Consequently the Hospitallers never achieved the same popular appeal and acclaim as the Templars. Unfortunately the tenets of monastic life were soon forgotten, and resentment and jealousy grew.

The two Orders attended every important meeting concerning the kingdom of Outremer; since both were very influential and needed to advance their own causes. The Templars were purported to support the Barons, the Hospitallers the monarchy, and this continually caused conflict. By 1179 the relationship between the two Orders had become so bad that on many occasions it led to bloodshed.

For three years after 1240, the Temple and the Hospital were at war with one another, due to disagreements over a treaty with the Moslems. They had running battles in the streets and laid siege to one another. One incident relates how they found themselves on opposite sides of a valley. From their vantage points both Orders fired volleys of arrows in an attempt to destroy each other.

It comes as no surprise that Jacques de Molay and the Grand Master of the Hospital were not interested in amalgamating the two Orders.

Religion, pride, jealousy and politics do not make easy bedfellows.

Despite this, the Templars and Hospitallers could still display solidarity outside warfare. At one point both Orders had a mutual dislike for one of the patriarchs of Jerusalem. The Hospitallers built a tower opposite the Church of the Holy Sepulchre which housed bells. When the patriarch began to speak the bells peeled out across the city drowning his voice. At the same time the Templars specifically used the closed doors of the church for archery practice, just to add to his problems!

The final insult to the Templars must have been when a papal decree was issued after their dissolution that gave all their possessions and land to the Hospitallers.

In closing this short explanation of the relationship between the two Orders, it must be understood that they were the mainstays of the crusader kingdoms – a matter often disregarded. Without them the kingdom would never have survived for the length of time it did. Conversely, it probably would have lasted longer had they presented a more united front.

THE HOLYLAND AT THE TIME OF THE CRUSADES

CYPRUS

Krak des Chevaliers

Ruad

TRIPOLI

Beirut

River Litani

MEDITERRANEAN SEA

Sidon

DAMASCUS

Tyre

ACRE

Safed

Haifa

Tiberias

SEA of GALILEE

Athlit

Nazareth

Caesarea

River Jordan

Arsuf

Nablus

Jaffa

JERUSALEM

Ascalon

DEAD SEA

Bethlehem

Gaza

0   20   40   60
Miles

DEMISE

𝒯he Crusades had lasted nearly 200 years, with the Holy Land being won or lost to both sides at various stages throughout the period.

In 1187 the city of Jerusalem had fallen to the armies of Saladin, never to be retaken again by Christendom. Now, due to bitter internal squabbling and the onslaught of Islam, the kingdom slowly started to collapse. The Christian kingdom moved its capital to the seaport of Acre.

Acre was a major trading centre, populated by peoples of all nations and denominations, with a thriving economic community of traders and businessmen.

With the fall of Jerusalem it became home to the Papal legate, the representative of the Pope, and a vast array of lords and princes. It was also the residence of the Grand Masters of the three major military orders: the Templars, Hospitallers, and the Teutonic knights.

Due to dwindling numbers of fighting men and the omnipresent threat from the Moslem kingdoms, pleas were made to Europe. In response the Pope sent reinforcements by sea. After a long period at sea, a few hundred peasants from Lombardy and Tuscany disembarked at Acre. They had not been paid and after three days had become jealous of the wealth they saw around them. Drunkenness and rioting followed, climaxing with the rape and murder of any Moslem, or anyone who looked similar, that they could find.

News always travels fast, especially if it is bad. The Sultan of Egypt, Qalawun, received the news with anger and hate. He demanded that the offenders be delivered to him for justice. This was placed before the ruling Council of Acre. The Grand Master of the Templars, William de Beujeu, who enjoyed a secret correspondence with Qalawun, agreed. Here we can see first hand the diplomatic links enjoyed by the Order and the Islamic world. De Beujeu would have readily agreed to this proposal since it made good political sense, essential for the survival of the Christian kingdom. But he was laughed at by a complacent Council, who accused him of being a traitor, and who arrogantly refused the demands of the Sultan.

Qalawun vowed a bloody revenge on the Christians. Again through the diplomatic channels, orchestrated by himself, de Beujeu received a message that Qalawun would not wreak vengeance if every citizen of Acre paid him one sequin, value approx. £7.70. De Beujeu again approached the Council with Qalawun's offer. Once again the offer was refused, and de Beujeu called a traitor.

In answer to their reply, Qalawun sent envoys to the Arab nations proposing a jihad (holy war), to rid the East of the Christians once and for all.

With news of an impending war, the Council of Acre sent messages once again to Europe begging for aid. It must have been the answer to many a prayer when the news of Qalawun's death was proclaimed. Unfortunately his son Al Ashraf Khali, made a vow to his dying father to continue the destruction of the Christian kingdom.

On the 5th of April 1291, the citizens of Acre were bewildered to see the enemy outside the city walls, vastly outnumbering them. The siege began.

As reinforcements from Europe arrived, Khali ordered the bombardment of the city walls to increase. During this period both the Hospitallers and Templars mounted a series of unsuccessful clandestine attacks. The two Orders had finally come together. Their hatred of one another had become legendary. Now they fought side by side in a last ditch attempt to survive. During the fighting the Grand Master of the Hospitallers was badly wounded and had to be evacuated by sea. The Grand Master of the Templars, William de Beujeu, died in battle from an arrow wound.

With the imminent fall of the city, the inhabitants began to flee via the sea. Theobald Gaudin, the Commander of the Temple, was ordered to leave with its treasure. Escorted by a small group of knights, and under cover of the night, Gaudin sailed for Sidon.

On the 8th of May, all that remained in Christian hands was the Temple. Three days later, Khali offered terms of surrender. It now appeared that the remaining Christians would be allowed to live. Khali's envoys were sent to the fortress. In response to acceptance of the terms, the Sultan's pennant was raised over the battlements. Shortly afterwards, the envoys returned with an escort of Moslem soldiers to complete the signing of the necessary documents. When the soldiers entered the Temple, the Moslem soldiers began to sexually abuse the women and children who had taken refuge within. The Templars retaliated, killing the envoys and all the Moslem soldiers. Their bodies were then thrown over the ramparts, the Sultan's flag torn down, and the Beauséant raised.

Khali then offered new terms. He invited the Mareschal of the Templars, Peter de Sevrey, to the Moslem lines to negotiate. De Severy and a small group of knights left the Temple to consider the new terms. When they arrived at the Moslem encampment they were set upon and tied up. All of them were dragged to within sight of the besieged Temple and beheaded. The defenders now realised all was lost and it would be a bitter fight to the end. Khali ordered his sappers to mine beneath the Temple walls.

Ten days after the Temple had been surrounded, the final assault began. As the enemy advanced across the fallen walls, the sappers had done their job too well. The beams they had set to uphold the mined structure collapsed under the weight of armour and troops. There was an almighty roar as the walls and the Temple fell, killing everyone. At last it was over.

On the 18th of May 1291 the city of Acre had fallen, and the crusaders were finally beaten, never to return. This was the beginning of the end for the Order of Knights Templar.

The remaining Templars of Outremer swiftly elected Theobald Gaudin as the new Grand Master. He left for Cyprus one night, since he had been given responsibility for the Order's treasure. There he hoped to consolidate the Eastern power base of the Order. The remainder found their way to Tortosa where they tried to beat off the attacking Mamelukes. But Tortosa was not able to sustain a siege. Very shortly the Templars retreated to an island two miles away called Ruad. From here, and for the next eleven years, the last Eastern garrison of the Order of Knights Templar held out.

Two years later Gaudin died and Jacques de Molay was elected in his place. He had loyally served as a warrior in the East for twenty eight years. An outspoken and highly critical man of about sixty three years of age, with a very narrow view on life and the role of the Order, he appears to have been a myopic fundamentalist with a very forceful and convincing manner. In conjunction with his poor foresight and diplomatic skills, de Molay was the worst type of person to steer the Order through the forthcoming troubles.

In 1302, the remnants of the Knights Templar in Outremer evacuated the island of Ruad. Without a kingdom and pilgrims to protect, their reason for existence had been removed.

In France, political intrigue began to work against the Order without its knowledge. Philip le Bel, the Capetian king of France who believed his ascension to the throne was ordained by divine right, was desperate. As a result of warring with England, he owed money. One of his creditors was the Temple.

Philip was described as sharp and strong willed. His face, although handsome (hence the name le Bel), revealed none of his emotions. He instinctively knew how others would behave in a given situation. Philip was a brilliant manipulator and skilled in deception, believing strongly in his role as Godhead and absolute monarch. He ruled coldly, deliberately by fear, through a network of Machiavellian ministers.

Philip had one real love, his wife, Jeanne. When she died in 1305, Philip is believed to have applied to join the Knights Templar. For some unknown reason, he was refused and this fuelled Philip's simmering resentment of the Order.

Philip, despite the loss of the Holy Land, was convinced of his divine role, and believed that it was only a matter of time before another crusade was called to regain the lost kingdom. He picked on a plan to amalgamate the two most powerful Military Orders of the time, the Templars and Hospitallers. Philip saw himself as the Grand Master of this combined Order, taking the title of Rex Bellator (the Warrior King). If he succeeded then, by right, his properties would be totally exempt from any form of taxation – thus ending his financial troubles. With this new position he also envisaged gaining land throughout Europe; in time ascending to his rightful place as the king of all Christendom, when Jerusalem was reconquered.

He had one problem, and that was to convince the two Military Orders. Jacques de Molay, the twenty third Grand Master of the Templars, saw the dangers of a combined Order and refused. The Master of the Hospitallers was not interested.

During this period Philip had tripled the cost of living in France, which had resulted in riots in Paris. He fled to the security of the Temple and for three days Philip took refuge with the Templars whilst the mob butchered and burned. Philip had time to think. Experiencing the wealth, power, and relative safety of the Order that had refused to admit him, did nothing to dampen the humiliation he already felt.

Shortly afterwards, having dealt with one group of creditors, the Lombards (money lenders from Lombardy), Philip, swiftly and without warning, confiscated all Jewish property and money. He had only one main creditor left, the Temple. Philip now plotted to seize the Templar wealth and bring about the downfall of the Order.

There was a civil servant called Guillaume de Nogaret in the employ of the king, adept in the underhand dealings of mediaeval politics. De Nogaret came from the south of France, an area that had suffered at the hands of crusading armies. St Bernard had preached holy war on the area due to the influence of Cathar teachings and its popularity over the established church. Although the teachings were based on Christianity, the Cathars believed in dualism and that all life was evil. Their priests were very committed and were seen to preach and practice their beliefs. The Catholic priests in the region had become corrupted, disillusioning the local population. The result was that Catharism became a threat. The resulting war (known as the Albigensian Crusade) was bloody in the extreme. The Templars played their part, albeit not in a military one, as was to be expected. De Nogarets' parents, being Cathars, both died in the conflict. It is worth noting that one of the main persecutors of the Cathars during this crusade were the Cistercians.

Philip had used him on a previous occasion before the fall of the Templars, to overthrow Pope Boniface VIII. On that occasion he had prepared allegations of heresy, sorcery, sodomy and consorting with a personal demon. These allegations had been compounded by accusations that Boniface's wealth had been obtained illegally. The result was the Pope's death, but there was such a public outcry that de Nogaret was excommunicated.

Philip now ordered this excommunicated servant to turn his attentions to the Templars, and strangely enough there is a somewhat familiar ring to the indictment.

The first phase of the operation was the placing of twelve spies into twelve Preceptories throughout France. Each was initiated into the Order. To further aid the plot, an expelled Knight Templar was found. He was willing to talk of witchcraft, sodomy and heresy conducted during the initiation rites of the Order.

One last reference to de Nogaret's formula – he repeated exactly the same allegations against a high ranking noble some years after the arrest of the Templars. He succeeded yet again.

On the renowned Friday 13th of October 1307, sealed orders were opened by Philip's Seneschals throughout France, instructing that all Templars be arrested. All but between twelve and twenty four of the 3,000 French Templars were promptly placed in prison. Records show that the prisons all over France were filled to overflowing. The execution of Philip's orders gave rise to the still current superstition that Friday 13th is unlucky.

One might speculate as to why the might of this fighting Order of monks, so expert in warfare from nearly two centuries of conflict with the Saracen, did not rise and defend itself. The answer to this is simple. It can be deduced from records of those arrested and tried and also from the break-up of the Templars after the fall of Acre. Bearing in mind that the whole western operation was purely to supply the eastern fighting force, most of the Templars in France were workers from the Order's lands; farm labourers, blacksmiths, shepherds and the like. As such, they were illiterate and ill informed. Moreover, the need for warriors had diminished since the fall of the Holy Land. Time and circumstance had changed the organisation into a business concern. The Order had become old and complacent; tinged with arrogance, it had failed to take note of, or to take seriously, the wind of change. Those arrested on that morning were not a vast army of warriors but a largely illiterate brotherhood of peasants, artisans and ageing monks.

The Templars at this point may have thought that they were on relatively safe ground since they were protected by the Holy See. Unfortunately the Pope, Clement V, was avaricious and spineless. His initial rise to power had been through the influence of his family and he owed his position to Philip. Clement knew the "nature of the Beast" and remembered the fate of both Boniface and Benedict, the Pope before him, who had died from severe stomach pains. Despite the odd grumble, he was under the control of Philip.

Torture began under the supervision of the Dominicans, the form and severity of which had never been known before. Their merciless ministrations earned them the nickname of "Dogs of the Lord" (Domine Canes)! One knight attended his trial with his amputated feet in his hands. The thousands who were to die by the hands of the Inquisition in later generations had Philip le Bel to thank for being an initiator of such tortures.

In France approximately fifty four knights were executed in total as relapsed heretics. This was as a direct result of withdrawing their confessions. Philip had become concerned at the strength of the Templar defence council at the trial and needed to set an example to those being tried. Needless to say his plan worked. No more confessions were recanted. Twelve committed suicide during the interrogations, and others died during torture. It was only in France that the Templars confessed to the allegations of witchcraft, sodomy and heresy. In the rest of Europe the allegations were mostly ignored or very little action was taken.

Philip's plot to seize the Templar wealth failed since it was never recovered. It is surmised that Jacques de Molay, Grand Master of the Order, had word of the plot some weeks before its implementation and had the treasure removed by a horse drawn cart to the awaiting Templar fleet, which also vanished without trace. More likely, the vast majority of the wealth did not consist of physical money, but was just bonds, receipts and written promises.

The Order was dissolved by papal decree in 1312.

Finally, on 14th March 1314, Jacques de Molay was taken out to publicly confess the sins of the Order, but instead declared its innocence. Geoffrey de Charney, Preceptor of Normandy, made a similar declaration. Both men were burnt to death on the small island of Javiaux by the Isle de Paris. Cured wood was used for the fires to ensure that the victims would not asphyxiate in the smoke but roast to death. Philip le Bel watched the death of the two knights.

Despite the posting of sentries throughout the night, a small group of monks swam across the Seine and searched through the smouldering coals. They swam back with the charred remains of de Molay and de Charney in their mouths.

Legend has it that Jacques de Molay cursed Pope Clement, Philip le Bel and the French royal family from the flames, demanding that they should join him and answer before God for their sins.

Thirty three days after the executions Clement died from a protracted, agonising illness. He was followed in the November by Philip, as a result of a riding accident (de Nogaret had died a year before in 1313). The Capetians kings, as a result, became known as "The Accursed Kings".

In 1793 the king of France, Louis XVI, the last legitimate Capetian, was imprisoned in the Temple of Paris. On a cold January morning he was taken to his place of execution. As the blade of the guillotine severed his head from his neck it was said that a man ran from the crowd to dip his kerchief in the king's blood, shouting that Jacques de Molay had finally been avenged.

The allegations made against the Order of Knights Templar have never been proved.

CONCLUSION

The romance of the Middle Ages casts an aura of mystery around the Templars. They were a product of their time, an insular organisation made even more powerful by wealth and military power, envied by kings and the Church alike.

It was a body capable of exerting its influence from England to the Baltic States, and from the wilderness of Palestine to the forests of France. Groups of knights meeting in their own sanctified territory, within the bounds of many countries, spread over great expanses of land. So powerful, rich and exclusive were they that it was guaranteed to generate hatred, jealousy and suspicion.

With a void created by the loss of records, and only a few details available about the Order's early life, the legends began. The Templars became guardians of the Holy Grail, the cup that Jesus Christ drank from at the Last Supper, and in which Joseph of Arimathea caught His blood as He hung on the Cross.

In later times it was said they protected the blood line of Christ, and more recently that they sought the Ark of the Covenant in Solomon's Temple when the Order began. Certainly the Templars did excavate the Temple on the Mount. Some say this was to find arcane wisdom, but it has been mooted that they discovered plans which taught the secrets of architecture and how to cut stone without the use of metal. The truth would appear to show that they were planning to build their own church upon the site.

Upon each Initiate the emphasis was on secrecy in any matters concerning the Rule and Chapter meetings. From this came a belief that there was a hidden agenda concealed from the uninitiated. This in turn led to allegations of witchcraft and secret knowledge. However, when looking at any organisation, their secret of success is silence. In the world of finance, and from the military aspect, knowledge of decision-making could mean disaster. In the everyday world it could mean gossip. The individual generally takes great care of his privacy, and this was true of all the military orders. Secrecy was not unique to the Templars, but this factor is rarely mentioned as it would negate the emphasis. No matter how hard researchers try, no *Hidden Rule* or secret doctrine can be validated.

There is a document called "The Larmenius Charter", which came to light in Paris in about 1804. At the present time it is housed in Mark Masons Hall in London. This purports to prove a line of succession from Jacques de Molay, who wrote it whilst incarcerated, nominating a Knight Templar in Cyprus, Johannes Marcus Larmenius as his successor. The line ends conveniently in 1804. The document has never been tested by carbon dating or by having the inks analysed. It has been and is still the cause of much debate. However there are a number of glaring problems. There are few records of Larmenius in any credible Templar document, and furthermore, de Molay was illiterate. Moreover, it has never been confirmed that the Templars ever used the cipher it has been written in. When deciphered the text would appear not to be in the Latin of the era in which it is purported to have been written. Due to his circumstances de Molay would not have been able to convene a Chapter meeting to ratify such a decision.

The document came to prominence at a time when, in the wake of the first French Revolution, there were many popular ideas linking events in France to clandestine organisations, especially Freemasonry and the Templars. It also coincided with an upsurge of interest in the ideals of the new masonic Christian degrees, Knight Templar being one of them.

In conversation with many people, and reading various authors on the subject, one comes across many sweeping statements. Apart from the assumption that Freemasonry was born from the demise of the Temple, there is another. There is an "accepted fact" that their initiation rites involved acts of sexuality, due to a natural evolution, i.e., warrior monks living together for long periods of time. But again this is conjecture based on rumour and the indictment. Prior to the fall of Acre and up to the indictment, no allegations of heresy or sodomy had ever been levelled against the Templars. Interestingly enough, the only Order that had ever been accused of heresy were the Hospitallers. In 1238 Pope Gregory had admonished the Hospitallers of Acre as it had come to light that some of the brethren were indulging in heretical practices and some were keeping brothels. The Templars, however, were only admonished for their lax attitude with regards their primary objectives. There is a tendency to forget the strength of their Christian belief. To understand the Templar, it must be understood that he was a very ordinary individual during an extraordinary epoch. When this period had passed he became surplus to the needs of Christendom and was therefore expendable.

The Templars were accused of blasphemy, sodomy, heresy, witchcraft, idolatry, and anything that would ensure their ultimate eradication. They were accused of worshipping a demon called Baphomet, not too dissimilar to the word Mohamet, the Arabic for Master. In the records of the trial it shows that the head/skull of a female was discovered amongst their belongings. Considering they were the guardians of Christian relics in the Holy Land, this is not too surprising.

There has been speculation concerning the Shroud of Turin. Some sources say it was a relic which the Templars held. To qualify this, the name of the family which delivered the shroud to the world was de Charney (the family name of the last preceptor of Normandy). However Malcolm Barber, of Reading University, puts forward a sound argument that it was highly unlikely that the shroud was ever in the possession of the Templars. Part of his argument stems from the fact there is no conclusive proof that the family de Charney were related in any way to the last preceptor of Normandy, except by name (much in the same way that the author George Eliot is no relation to T. S. Eliot). He further adds that the nature of the organisation was not to keep their relics secret. The Templar understood the power of any religious artefact when faced with the superstitious nature of the general populace. In fact one of the most holy of relics was the True Cross, of which they were the custodians. The Templars utilised this as much as possible as a propaganda machine and rallying point. If they did have the true representation of the Body of Christ, why would they keep it secret and not use it to the benefit of themselves and Christendom?

Taking into account the records of the interrogation, what becomes abundantly clear is that the confessions were obtained by the use of torture and leading questions. The answers were never given by the victim of their own volition but always in a manner which would satisfy the demands of their interrogators. When dealing with any account of the supposed practices of the Order as a result of the trial, consideration must be given to the nature of the indictment and its reason. It was to destroy the Templars.

It is difficult to believe that men who sacrificed everything, fought and died in their thousands in defence of the Holy Christian faith, suddenly denied all that they had previously stood for. The men who protected the highways of Europe and Palestine may have been guilty of arrogance, avarice and ambition, but they were not magicians, heretics or sodomites. A few may have strayed from the path, but not all.

The Knights Templar set the ideals for Christian chivalry. Albeit largely illiterate, the Order created the foundation of the modern day banking system, which in turn created wealth for princes and kings. They expanded learning and knowledge, opening up diplomatic links between the Christian and the Moslem worlds, at the same time stopping the spread of Islam throughout Europe. This resulted in the creation of the finest and most comprehensive intelligence system the world had ever known. Apart from banking, one of their major cultural legacy to us is Gothic architecture, which they actively encouraged and which is still prominent throughout Christendom. This ultimately changed the face of mediaeval Europe and heralded the advent of modern day buildings and design.

Despite what appears to be a deliberate campaign waged to silence and discredit them by the established church of the era, their influence still resounds today.

The downfall of the Templars was brought about by the loss of Outremer, their own arrogant complacency and the greed of one man, Philip le Bel.

There is no mystery about the Order of the Knights of the Temple. They were a monastic order of monks from the upper, middle and lower echelons of feudal Europe, dedicated to the worship of Christ and the protection of Christendom from heresy and Islam. Time has been their enemy in the respect of reputation and legend. Through the centuries there have been various groups who have claimed a right of succession from Jacques de Molay. But, again, with no foundation. The dangers of these organisations are self-evident, especially with the example of the mass killings associated with "The Solar Temple" based mainly in Canada and Switzerland. Their self-styled Grand Master claimed this right; their dogma based upon a "Hidden Rule".

The knights, sergeants and serving brothers of the real Order would no doubt be saddened and horrified to see the bastardisation of the fraternity they held so dear. The irony is, if the Templars were still in existence today then a crusade would most definitely be called against such heresies. The Beauséant would be raised and thousands of warriors would once again chant the refrain "Non nobis, Domine, non nobis, sed Tuo Nomini da gloriam!".

So, my friend, as you move sadly up the stairway of time take a glance behind and, as the mists close over the past, remember the thousands who died in that brown, barren wasteland with its perpetual dust, searing heat and scorching sun, and give thanks to them for their sacrifice.

THOUGH STRIFE AND TURMOIL ALL AROUND,
HE STANDS HARD BUT STEADY ON THE GROUND.
BY THE CAPTAIN'S TENT TWO BANNERS FLY,
BLACK, WHITE AND VEXULLUM BELLI.
HARK, CAN YOU HEAR THAT DISTANT CALL,
FROM AGES PAST TO ONE AND ALL?
A ROAR THAT THUNDERS FROM TEMPLE MOUNT
"ENOUGH MY BROTHERS, Á BEAUSÉANT . . .

Á BEAUSÉANT!"

Paul Ivison

NOTES

*A*ccording to one major source at the time, there were about 9,000 Templar Manors across Europe – all exempt from taxation.

In France there were approximately 3,000 Templars. Between twelve and twenty four escaped, either from receiving prior warning, poor security by the arresting soldiers or just good fortune. It was recorded that the prisons were overflowing that morning of Friday 13th of October 1307 throughout France.

In Paris, 138 Templars were interrogated. 15 were knights, 17 were priests, 41 were sergeants and serving brothers. The rest were unrecorded rank.

Of the 15 knights:

Jacques de Molay   Grand Master
Hugues de Pairaud   Visitor of France
Geoffrey de Charney   Preceptor of Normandy

and the

Preceptors of   Acquitaine
               Rheims
               Cyprus

BIBLIOGRAPHY

BARBER, Malcolm	Trial of the Templars The New Knighthood The Origins of the Temple 　　(Studia Monastica, vol 12, 1970) The Templars and the Turin 　　Shroud (Shroud Spectrum 　　International 1983)
BARBER, Richard	The Knight and Chivalry
BRADFORD, E.	The Sword and the Scimitar
BROOKE, Christopher	General History of Europe 962-1154
BURMAN, Edward	Templars, Knights of God
BUTLER	Lives of the Saints
DOWLEY, Tim	History of Christanity
EDBURY, Peter W. ROWE, John Gordon	William of Tyre
ECO, Umberto	Foucault's Pendulum
FOREY, A. J.	The Templars in the Corona de Aragon
FOSS, Michael	Chivalry
HOPKINS, Andrea	Knights
HOWARTH, Stephen	The Knights Templar

JOIN-LAMBERT, Michel	Jerusalem
LAWRENCE, T. E.	Crusader Castles
LEES, Beatrice A.	Records of the Templars in England in the Twelfth Century
LINCOLN, Henry BAIGENT, Michael LEIGH, Richard	Holy Blood and the Holy Grail The Temple and the Lodge
NICHOLSON, Helen	Saints or Sinners? (History Today, December, 1994)
OXFORD	Book of Saints Dictionary of the Christian Church
PARTNER, Peter	The Knights Templar and Their Myth
PAYNE, Robert	The Dream and the Tomb (A history of the Crusades)
PENGUIN	Book of Saints
ROBINSON, John	Born in Blood Dungeon, Fire and Sword (The Knights Templar in the Crusades)
RUNCIMAN, Steven	A History of the Crusades
SINCLAIR, Andrew	The Sword and the Grail
UPTON WARD, J. M.	The Rule of the Templars
WILLIAMSON, J. Bruce	The History of the Temple, London
WISE, Terence SCOLLINS, Richard	The Knights of Christ

APPENDIX I

CHECKLIST FOR KNIGHTS JOINING THE ORDER OF THE TEMPLE

✠

Name:

Date of Birth:

1.	Catholic Faith	☐
2.	Legitimately Born	☐
3.	Not Married	☐
4.	Not in Holy Orders	☐
5.	Noble Birth	☐

✠

APPENDIX II

EQUIPMENT CHECK

1. One (1) ceremonial mantle-red cross .... ☐

2. Two (2) shirts .... ☐

3. One (1) tunic – long sleeve .... ☐

4. Two (2) pairs of shoes .... ☐

5. Two (2) pairs of britches .... ☐

6. One (1) under coat – padded (*Gambeson*) .... ☐

7. One (1) long surcoat (open at front running from waist down) with red cross .... ☐

8. One (1) cape .... ☐

9. Two (2) mantles .... ☐

10. One (1) leather belt .... ☐

11. One (1) cap .... ☐

12. Two (2) towels .... ☐

13. Two (2) blankets .... ☐

14. One (1) suit of mail (*Hauberk*) .... ☐

15. One (1) pair of leggings .... ☐

16. One (1) pair of prick spurs .... ☐

17. One (1) sword .... ☐

18.   One (1) lance...☐
19.   One (1) Turkish mace (with spike).......................☐
20.   One (1) shield...☐
21.   One (1) steel helmet ....☐
22.   Two (2) knives...☐
23.   One (1) eating knife ....☐
24.   Three (3) horses ....☐
25.   One (1) rolled matress for campaigning................☐

✠

Signed as issued:

Print name:

Rank:

Date of issue:

APPENDIX III

EQUIPMENT CHECK FOR SERGEANTS AND SERVING BROTHERS

1. One (1) black tunic – red cross front and back.. ☐

2. One (1) black/brown mantle .... ☐

3. One (1) domed cap of iron................................. ☐

4. One (1) coat of mail – sleeveless .... ☐

5. One (1) pair of hose .... ☐

6. One (1) horse (sergeants only).......................... ☐

7. One (1) shield .... ☐

8. One (1) sword .... ☐

9. Two (2) daggers .... ☐

10 One (1) spear/lance.. ☐

APPENDIX IV

DAILY ROUTINE TO BE STRICTLY ADHERED TO

4am: Rise and attend horses.

         Return to bed.

6am: Attend   Mass
                    Prime
                    Tierce
                    Sext

         Training and horse grooming

12 Noon: Dinner:

Knights will be served first. There will be a choice of cooked meats. **There will be no fasting**. There will be complete silence throughout the meal whilst the chaplain reads from the holy scriptures.

3pm: Nones.

6pm: Vespers.

         Supper.

9am: Compline (after which there will be served a glass of wine and water).

         Instructions for the following day.

         Attend to horses.

12 Midnight: Matins, then to bed in complete silence until 4am.

By order of the Grand Master.

A BRIEF CHRONICLE OF THE RISE AND FALL OF THE KNIGHT TEMPLAR IN LONDON

After the success of the Council of Troyes (which would now appear to be 13th January 1129, due to an anomaly in the calendar) the first Grand Master of the Templars, Hugues de Payens, went on a recruitment campaign. Within the year he travelled through France and onto Normandy, the property of King Henry I of England. With Henry's full support de Payens made his way across the Channel to England. The chosen headquarters for the fledgling Order was London. Their first House was built in Holborn, to the north of what is now known as Chancery Lane (previously called New Street believed to have been built by the Templars). The Chapter house included a church, built in "the round" to emulate the church of the Holy Sepulchre in Jerusalem, using stones imported from Caen in Normandy for its construction. As the new Preceptory was to be the headquarters of the English, Scottish and Irish branches of the Order, no expense was to be spared and shortly the area of ownership grew in size and opulence.

The southern point of their boundary was the river Thames and the northern what is now known as Fleet Street and the Strand. The areas east and west are not very accurate but it is believed that they were within the bounds known as White Friars. Across the Thames they rented a section of "Wideflete" from the monks of Bermondsey (opposite the present day site of the Temple). Beyond the road from Fleet Street on the city side of Chancery Lane (New Street), they built two forges: one forge on the west side and one on the east side of the present day site of St Dunstan's church, primarily for the requirements of a martial force. Once the Order had consolidated its foothold, recruitment began in earnest. At the onset there were only knights of noble birth but soon they took on freemen as serving brothers to attend on the knights.

The knights were closely associated with the royal court from the start, and soon the Temple became a centre of the affairs of state and church alike. The Master of the Temple became as powerful as any lord of a demesne, frequently used as an ambassador to other kingdoms and feuding subjects. They had the power of the papacy and military force to their advantage. The Master of the Temple (officially known as the ***Magister Militiae Templi in Anglia***), Richard of Hastings, played a very important part during the quarrel of Henry II and Thomas Becket, in trying to placate both parties. The Templars were of great support to King John during his reign, who on many occasions sought refuge in Templar properties. He gave them the island of Lundy as a gift. In 1214 the Magna Carta was signed under duress by King John at Runnymede. On this important constitutional document, the Master of the

Temple is mentioned within the introduction as one of the king's advisors.

The Order's banking skills came to the fore when they provided aid to English kings which further benefited the Order's status. One example is the support they gave to Richard Coeur de Lion during his successful crusade between 1190 and 1193. The centre of their banking was the New Temple in London, which had become their headquarters in 1161. From here they developed a system of national and international finance. The Templars are believed to have developed the first cheques for credit transfer.

With regards to the New Temple, it still exists and is open to the public, despite being hidden within the confines of the Inns of Court. It survived the Great Fire in 1666, and part of it was restored after being bombed in 1941 during the Blitz. Effigies of mediaeval knights lie poignantly in the centre of the round. Their dress and swords denote they are all warriors. Those with their legs crossed is an indication that they had been on crusade – and not that they were Templars, a popular misconception. To some this may be a slight disappointment, but what outweighs this is that one of the effigies is of William Marshall, the Earl of Pembroke. Marshall was the epitome of the chivalrous knight. A fitting place for the effigy of such a man to rest – within the church of those who set the ideals of Christian chivalry.

After the arrest of the French Templars, Philip le Bel sent a confidential clerk to the court of Edward II to expose the Templars and urge action against them. The English king and his court refused to believe the allegations. On 22nd November 1307 Pope Clement V issued a bull exhorting Edward with "caution and secrecy" to arrest all the Templars. As a result the warrants were issued on 20th December 1307 and dispatched throughout the land with orders that their contents should be kept secret until they had been executed.

In England the warrants were executed over a three day period, from 9th to 11th January 1308. Despite being incarcerated the Templars were treated very well, and were given an allowance of 4d (1.5p) a day by a king who held them in high esteem. Questioning began between October and November 1309 under the umbrella of the Inquisition. Of the forty three Templars incarcerated at the church of the Holy Trinity in London, none confessed to any of the allegations. Torture had not been used at this stage. As a point of interest one of the knights was William Raven who had been accepted into the Order at Templecombe in 1305. Under questioning he gave an account of the initiation service, which revealed little that could be used in evidence against the Templars. Eventually, after pressure from the church and papacy, Edward gave permission for the inquisitors to use whatever methods they wished to extract their confessions. With the application of torture the process began to work and Templars started to confess. The trials were over by the 13th July 1309. English justice demanded that they should publicly confess. Those that were too old or fatigued as a result of their confinement or torture, could confess in a chapel at All Hallows near the Tower of London. After this they were to go to other Orders or monasteries throughout England in order to do their penance. The Master, William de la More, refused to admit to any of the allegations. His case was referred to the Papal Council at Vienne, but he died in the Tower in 1313 before a decision could be reached. William's guest, the Preceptor of Auvergne, was not so lucky; arrested at the same time, he also denied the allegations. The council at Vienne ordered that he be bound in double iron fetters and incarcerated in the worst prison available and be visited on a regular basis to convince him to confess. He died under these conditions, still refusing to confess.

In closing this very brief chronicle of the Templars in London, one or two observations come to mind. London was only a small part of their demesne. Other counties such as Scotland, Essex, Kent, Somerset, Cambridgeshire and Hertfordshire benefited from their development of rural pastures. Their largest concentration was in Yorkshire where large areas were reclaimed from marshland. Their expertise in land reclamation, their financial, political and military accomplishments meant the Templars were an important influence on the early development of England. Popular history tends to do them little justice, and will generally only concentrate on the allegations of Philip le Bel's indictment. Due to the belief in these allegations by the mediaeval church and papal pressure there appears to have been a concerted effort to push them wrongly into insignificance. There is a wealth of information still available about the Order, but one has to be selective in what one chooses to believe. The vast majority of Templar records were destroyed in Cyprus by the Ottomans when they invaded in 1571. This has inevitably led to supposition, which in the case of some authors is The Rule for selling books about the Order. The brothers of the Temple were a committed military, monastic order of monks who became a wealthy state within a state. Their primary objective was to retain their field force in the Levant (Outremer) for the protection of pilgrims, relics and the Holy Places of the Christian religion against Islam. In doing so the European administration was a quartermaster's store, no more no less, which became very wealthy due to the ability of the knights and brothers. Take away Philip's very questionable indictment, supposition and a degree of human frailty: and what is left?

Non nobis, Domine, non nobis, sed Tuo Nomini da gloriam!